Who's Picking Me Up from the Airport?

Who's Picking Me Up

from the

Airport?

and Other Questions Single Girls Ask

CINDY JOHNSON

ZONDERVAN®

ZONDERVAN

Who's Picking Me Up from the Airport?
Copyright © 2015 by Cindy Johnson

This title is also available as a Zondervan ebook.
Visit www.zondervan.com/ebooks.

Requests for information should be addressed to:

Zondervan, 3900 *Sparks Dr. SE, Grand Rapids, Michigan 49546*

Library of Congress Cataloging-in-Publication Data

Johnson, Cindy, 1981-
     Who's picking me up from the airport? : and other questions single girls ask /
Cindy Johnson. —
        pages   cm
        ISBN 978-0-310-34096-6 (softcover)
      1. Christian women — Religious life. 2. Single people — Religious life. 3. Dating
(Social customs) — Religious aspects — Christianity. I. Title.
    BV4527.J634 2015
    248.8'432 — dc23   2014040215

Published in association with literary agent Heidi Mitchell of D.C. Jacobson & Associates LLC, an Author Management Company www.dcjacobson.com

Cover design: *Dual Identity*
Interior design: *David Conn*

First printing December 2014 / Printed in the United States of America

For my mother, Alice,
the most beautiful person I know.
Please accept this token of gratitude
for your unconditional love, patience,
and licks from the cookie-dough beaters.
Thank you for always believing in me.
I love you!

Contents

Acknowledgments

All my love and gratitude to my dad, Mike, and my brothers, Tim, Mark, and Matt. I cringe thinking of the kind of guy I'd be tied to now if you four hadn't exemplified such great men. Thank you for your love, help, and friendship. You are my life's greatest joy!

A wholehearted "Cheers!" to my inspirational and lovely single friends/contributors/editors! I'm honored to share this phase of life with you, on and off paper. Thank you for bravely telling your stories. Listed in alphabetical order, so as to avoid hurt feelings (Is this what picking out bridesmaids feels like?): Amy, Brittany, Christina, Jody, Katie, Keturah, Laura, Linnsey, Melinda, Melody, Morgan, Stine, and Sullivan.

A special thanks to Alicia Streelman, Alyssa Firovanti, Bill and Katy White, Bree Minefee, Christine Bury, Davey, Greg and Sara Dolmage, Heather Carter, Jason and Emilie Brown, Jenni Johnson, Jon, Kayla Adams, Lori Johnson, and

Rob. Without your encouraging words and input, none of this would have happened. Thank you for supporting my journey.

To my wonderful agent, Heidi Mitchell, and everyone at D. C. Jacobson and Associates: thank you for believing in the message and in me. You have changed my life! To my incredible editor, Carolyn McCready, and the talented people at HarperCollins and Zondervan, thank you for the opportunity of a lifetime.

And last and least, to all my ex-boyfriends, who truly made this book possible.

XOXO,

Cindy

Introduction

If you met your husband at Christian college, this book is not for you. If you married someone you met on a missions trip, at summer camp, or in youth group, this book isn't for you. If you got married before the age of twenty-seven, have the +1 wedding date situation on lockdown, or wake up every day and think, "Yep, this is how I envisioned my life at this age," then this book is not for you. Of course, you are more than welcome to read it, and by all means buy it. But I'm telling you, you might not identify with it. Just like I don't understand the agony of losing sleep with a newborn, incorporating a man into my closet space, or handling a crazy mother-in-law, *you* might not resonate with *my* story either.

There are lots of Christian books written for wives and mothers. Trying to find something helpful for a single adult female? Forget it. And no, *I Kissed Dating Goodbye* and *Redeeming Love* do not count. Those books are great if you're debating how soon is too soon for the side hug, but they don't tell you how low is too low when trying on shirts to go out in on a Friday night. Nor do they warn you that the church's golden-boy worship leader might turn out to be a complete tool. Books like those certainly serve a purpose, but they don't meet me in my phase of life.

I know it's hard to believe, but when I began writing this book, it wasn't so I could broadcast to the world that Cindy Johnson is still single. I *never* wanted to be a spokeswoman for single women. I'm offended when my mom ever so slyly mentions that the speaker at our women's retreat isn't married or offers to pay for eHarmony as a Christmas gift. I'm totally worried this book will stick the final nail in my "she died alone" coffin. And yes, I'm afraid people will say things like, "Isn't that Cindy, the girl who can't find a husband, so she wrote a book?"

Thankfully, all that pressure is misguided. According to a US Census from 2010, men and women are waiting longer and longer to get married. The current median age for women is twenty-seven, and it's twenty-nine for men.[1] You are simply not the last single girl under the age of twenty-three on the planet. I continually meet women who are wondering why the heck they are still single and whether there are any decent men left. And more than pity, Christian cliches, or empty advice, what we all need is laughter and honest conversation about singleness. So I'm taking one for the team and attempting to provide some candid thoughts on the subject. If I do end up a spinster, you all owe me. Big time.

I chose to write this book as a gift for my single friends. They are beautiful, intelligent women who sometimes wake up afraid, frustrated, and disappointed. Turns out the best comfort, perhaps the only comfort, any of us can bring each other is friendship. My hope is that you'll find in this book someone who gets you. Someone else whose life has turned out far different than she thought it would.

I wish you and I could meet up and swap stories in person over coffee or a glass of wine. These pages will have to do in the meantime.

Most of all, I hope I leave you feeling there is nothing wrong with you.

Before we begin, I would like to make a few disclaimers, to help you get to know me better.

Number one, I am not ugly. Seriously. I get my eyebrows done and know to avoid kitten heels and light wash jeans. Also, I'm not a weirdo. I point this out because if *I* picked up this book, I'd definitely assume the author is a mess. I'd have already done a Google images search to confirm my suspicions. For all intents and purposes, I'm normal. (I should also mention that I'm not drop-dead gorgeous, crazy, or afraid of commitment either. Well, okay, I'm a little afraid of commitment, but we'll touch on that later.)

Number two, I don't live in some posh mountain home with my husband, two kids, and golden retriever. I live in Southern California and rent an overly decorated room (thank you, Pinterest) with other single girls who cycle out when they get engaged. I don't have pets or kids. I survive on lots of single-girl staples like Kashi cereal and overpriced coffee.

Number three, I can't answer questions like, "Where can I meet a man?" "Why do I know way more quality girls than quality guys?" and, "Why am I still single?" If I could speak to those, I'd probably be on the other side tormenting you with boring status updates about my "hubby." And if you're looking for answers to those questions in a book, you might want to rethink your strategy too.

Number four, this isn't some Christian book promising to change your life. At best, it will make you feel a little better about the one you already have. The coming pages are simply my story. I tell it so you'll know you are not alone and you're not single because of something you've done wrong. There is most likely nothing wrong with you. Period. Your church friends, extended family, and old college roommates may not know what to do with you, but if we met, I'm pretty sure we'd have a lot in common.

Number five, just for kicks: I don't easily trust people who consistently order salad instead of fries or claim to hate TV. I never give gifts accompanied by cards; I'm way too disorganized and cheap for that. I once learned the entire dance to "Men in Black" and performed it with my fellow lifeguards at Thousand Pines Christian Camp in high school. This may have been my peak.

Okay, that's enough to get us started. I look forward to being friends.*

---

*All the names in this book have been changed to protect the identities of my ex-boyfriends. Did it take great restraint not to use their real ones? You bet.
Also, you'll find letters from my friends at the beginning of each chapter. I gave them the option to use fake names, and they all chose to use their real ones. Which I think is pretty great. Be sure to thank them with a hug if you ever meet them.

Chapter 1

What I'm Working With

My Adolescent Dating Baggage

It does not do to dwell on dreams
and forget to live, remember that.

—Albus Dumbledore,
Harry Potter and the Sorcerer's Stone

Name: Melody
Age: 29
Occupation: Nonprofit Spokesperson
City: Newport Beach, California

— — —

Dear friend,

Let's just cut to the chase: heartbreak sucks. Like most of us, I've survived several, and I'm still finding my way through one as I write you.

When my mom was six months pregnant with me, she went to Vegas and married my dad. His cocaine addiction is mostly to blame for his leaving us shortly after I was born. He popped in a few times over the course of my childhood: always charming, always boasting sparkling promises he could never keep. He was my first real heartbreak.

My mom remarried when I was five, and her marriage meant I got a dad. I've been calling him Dad and using his last name since kindergarten. He officially adopted me when

I was eight. I believed he rescued me from becoming a girl with daddy issues.

For a long time, I thought my story was one of redemption, believing that all of my hard work to show God what a good kid I was paid off. For years, I was proud of my family and thought I'd escaped feeling the byproducts of my beginnings.

Then when I was in college, my mom and dad got divorced.

My third heartbreak.

My second heartbreak was wedged somewhere in the middle of the first two when I fell in love with an addict who walked out of my life without a goodbye. (But like I said, nothing about me had anything to do with my childhood. Obviously.) Maybe that's why the same addict boyfriend was also my fourth heartbreak, years later, when we decided to try a brutal round two.

My fifth heartbreak was at twenty-six — around when I was sure I had finally figured everything out. I found a good man who cared for my heart. He was honest, suffered no addictions, and was kind through and through. Unfortunately, he eventually changed his mind about what he wanted for our future. He couldn't shed much light on his decision, just told me all the things he loved about me, but that he didn't think we were meant to go the distance. This heartbreak turned out to be one of the worst, and I spent far longer than I care to admit trying to recover.

I'm betting that if this letter caught your attention, it's because you too know heartbreak better than you want to. I wish I knew a way around it, but instead, I hope you'll hear the comfort I find in the words of Paul: "Brothers and sisters, I do not consider myself yet to have taken hold of it. But one thing I do: Forgetting what is behind and straining toward what is ahead, I press on toward the goal to win the prize for which God has called me heavenward in Christ Jesus" (Phil. 3:13–14).

The word that gets me here is "straining." It's as if God recognizes that moving forward is painful and uncomfortable. It's met with the temptation to move backward instead, to return to something familiar, even if it's not good for you. Other times, the temptation will be to skip it altogether and find a distraction. The good news is that if you're feeling the strain, if your heart is breaking, that means you're moving forward. I know it doesn't feel like it, but that strain is a sign of your strength.

We were designed to heal. And our healing is designed to participate in the healing of others. God is using my story for a greater purpose, to point me and others closer to him. I've seen him do it with all my heartbreaks.

What I want you to know is that if this part of your story hurts right now, I'm so sorry. I wish I could hug you and cry with you and that we could laugh our way through it. But mostly, I wish I could tell you how brave you are and that your healing is coming. And that with it you will do beautiful things.

Thanks for letting me share with you.

Melody

- -

The first boy I ever liked was Mark-Paul Gosselaar. I realized something was different when I got embarrassed while watching episodes of *Saved by the Bell* with my family in the room. *Can they tell? Does everyone know I like him? I should probably say that I think* Full House *is a way better show . . . Yeah, that will throw them off for sure.*

In middle school, I had my first boyfriend, Brad. I felt so cool during lunch when he'd come and stand by me. He had this beautiful blond hair and pretty blue eyes. My friends were jealous. I could tell. We had a brief, noncommunicative affair that ended three weeks later when I dumped him to get out of buying him a Christmas present. There was no way I was telling my mom we needed to go shopping for a boy at school. I'd rather die.

I didn't have another boyfriend till I was twenty-seven.

I grew up in a very small town in California called Banning. This is vital information because it means I had very few opportunities for real life crushes. There were exactly nine decent boys in my high school. My dad was the senior pastor of the main church in town, so that left only four boys who were still willing to take on the challenge of dating a preacher's daughter. The fact that I also have three brothers scared away the remaining and left me with zero. Zero boys to date.

Looking back, I'm not sure it would've mattered anyway. In middle school, I wore a lot of Anchor Blue baggy striped shirts and lipstick in the shade of "raisin." In high school I opted for Roxy everything and thought it was cool not to wear makeup. At no point did anyone bother to pull me aside and remind me that guys like girls who look like girls. *Where were you on that one, Mom?*

There were some guys in high school who liked me, but only really weird ones—Boy Scouts and the occasional gang-banger with a romantic heart. There were a handful of cute Mormon boys (on account of our shared values), but they were off limits. I'm sure a few others here and there thought about asking me out but decided it wasn't worth their time since I was a proud card-carrying member of the abstinence crew.

My one major high school crush (who didn't live in TV or a book) was Andy. Another blue-eyed number with a big smile. My Andy saga started in second grade when he showed up at our house to play with my older brother. I tried to win him over with the old game of saying mean things to him, in what I can only imagine was a really high-pitched voice, while practicing my New Kids on the Block moves in his line of sight.

He never responded to any of this.

But I did once catch a glimmer of hope when I was sixteen. Somehow my friend Carrie's boyfriend managed to rope him into a double date to our town's carnival. I couldn't contain myself, I was so excited. My whole life had led up to this very moment. I remember everyone in my family was eating dinner in the dining room, except for me, because, you know, I had a date. As my pickup time of 5:00 turned into 5:20, to 5:30, I began to worry. Carrie finally called around 6:00 and said, "Cindy, we can't find Andy. I'll pick you up."

Walking through the dining room with my family watching me get stood up was one of my most humiliating moments. This never would have happened to my brothers. Girls in our town would have killed to date them, and I couldn't even get a date to show up.

I was confused. All of the youth group talks about making lists of "What I'm Praying for in a Future Husband" had led me to believe it would be a fairly easy deal. Get the right list, get the right guy. Simple. Creating the perfect must-haves was my part. Dropping him in my life in an exciting and movielike way was God's part. Obviously. If I carefully lived up to my future husband's ideal-wife list—some hybrid of a Proverbs 31 woman and a super sexy model who stayed quiet—God would bring me my soul mate and we'd live happily ever after.

No one told me I might have to date around, be rejected or disappointed. I wasn't sure how to file Andy's rejection into the easy and beautiful storyline I'd been sold. *Where have I gone wrong? Is it something I did?* Somewhere inside, I started to believe that God worked love out for those worth loving. The fact that it didn't go well for me meant something was wrong with me. The good people get chosen. The rest of us don't.

After Andy, with little to guide me out of my embarrassment, I began formulating a game plan that consisted of pretending I didn't want to date anyone, while secretly hoping some guy would chase after me, proving I was worthy. I would give no sign of liking a guy until I was absolutely sure he was in. For his entire life. It was my zero-risk plan.

And what better place to try this plan out than at a godly girl's man buffet—Christian college. In my head, there would be an endless supply of guys waiting to meet someone just like me. My dating pool would finally contain the kind of guys my dad would allow me to date. When I arrived, I found instead a bunch of over-emotive boys whose mothers had loved them too much. I was pretty disappointed with the selection.

Most of them seemed to think God would deliver a virgin Jessica Alba if they went to church regularly and didn't sleep with their girlfriends. Apparently the guys were sold some bad dating advice along the way too.

They weren't all bad guys, of course. It just took some effort to sort the dateable guys from the nondateable. If you busted out your guitar and sang worship songs unnecessarily, I wasn't interested. If you asked me to grab coffee and "share my testimony," I wasn't interested. If you blamed your last breakup on God, I ran for the hills. If you surfed and didn't know I existed, I secretly timed all my meals so I'd run into you in the cafeteria.

Unfortunately, this behavior kept me out of any real relationships and led to a few inappropriate friendships. Inappropriate friendships run rampant at Christian colleges. Warn your daughters. This is when you and a boy spend lots and lots of time hanging out. You grow very close emotionally and spiritually, but not physically. Hooking up meant you had to have a DTR (determining the relationship). Most guys prefered to keep it vague. Less responsibility. And since your inappropriate guy friend never declares what he is actually doing with you, the ball is in your court to make it a "more than friend" kind of thing. Only you can never be sure that's what he wants, because he never makes it clear.

This sends you on a massive crazed case of unsolved mystery where you must draw your own conclusions with only clueless girlfriends from your dorm as sounding boards. "He said God told him I should go on a dating fast for six months. That means he doesn't want me dating anyone else, right?" "He turned down that girl from his biology class. That's because we are a thing, right?" "He invited me to Chili's while his parents are in town. He is in love with me, RIGHT?!"

Lots of girls were obsessed with getting married right out of college. (The whole "ring by spring" thing was alive and well at my school.) I wasn't. And neither was my friend Jody. She and I met after class our freshmen year. Together, we decided it was best to have at least four boyfriends before graduating and travel and have a career before settling down.

I thought I had found my perfect first boyfriend when I met Eric, with whom I had an IF with during most of college. We met early on and became friends right away. The kind of close friends who spend lots of time together but never address any feelings. It was frustrating and confusing. Whether intentionally or unintentionally, he got all the benefits of a girlfriend (someone to leave him a voice-mail message before a big presentation, someone to listen to him vent, a shoulder to cry on) without any commitment.

Eric and I kept our thing going right up until the day he called me to catch up over the summer. We chatted for an hour or so while I pictured us holding hands and walking campus that next fall. He eventually said, "Oh, hey, I don't think I told you, I started dating this girl from home over break and I'm thinking about proposing!" In perfect IF form, I finally got my answers. I finally knew for sure how he felt, because it was over. He liked someone else. And wanted to MARRY HER.

Don't worry, it got better. Jody came to the wedding as my date that next summer.

You'd think I'd have learned my lesson, but unfortunately I repeated the same cycle with two more guys after Eric. Since they weren't boyfriend-girlfriend relationships, I never spent any real time reflecting on how I felt. I never asked myself why I allowed someone to treat me like that in the first place.

One day, I came to the conclusion that the embarrassment I felt over Mark-Paul Gosselaar was the same embarrassment that kept me from buying Brad a Christmas gift all those years ago. It was that same feeling that allowed me to linger in a crush for years. It's how I rationalized letting guys get to know the best parts of me without ever having to be responsible to me. Jody eventually pointed it out to me when she said, "Cin, you never want to be the fool."

How right she was. I never wanted to be the one who put her heart on the line. More than finding love or expecting guys to treat me the way I deserved to be treated, I didn't want to experience rejection because I didn't want to have to wonder if there was something wrong with me. As long as no one technically turned me down, I could go on thinking I was a catch. As long as I never pushed anyone to choose me, I wouldn't have to face them if they said no.

After college, I made the shift I believe all girls have to make for themselves: you have to know you are a catch regardless of your relationship status. I always liked myself, but I still needed a guy to prove my worth.

Once I realized how wrong that thinking is, I stopped giving time to friendships with males I was interested in. If they were going to get to know me, they were going to have to date me. I was worth it, and I needed another guy friend like I needed a hole in my head. There was enough gray area to navigate in my twenties; I didn't need it in my relationships. Guys take a ton of our emotional time and effort. I decided if they weren't adding to my life, they were holding me back.

Now when I meet a guy I want to ask me out, I say to myself, "He should ask me out." And a lot of the time he does. Things didn't change because I suddenly looked so much better. I wasn't funnier, better at flirting, or nicer. I believe their responses changed as a result of the change in me. When I finally and confidently owned my beauty and worth, they did too.

The vibe you and I put out when we believe the man standing in front of us would be lucky to spend time with us actually makes a difference. Before every date, Jody and I always tell each other, "You are the prize." It may sound a little cheesy, but when you and I know our worth, it sends a message to us and the guys we date about what he can and can't get away with.

I wish I'd known earlier in life that as women, we hold a lot of power. Some guys will try to get away with whatever you let them get away with. Even the good ones are testing the boundaries in some form. It's okay to put yourself out there and get rejected, especially if it saves you from confusion and wasted time. Especially if it protects you from giving a guy something for free he was never planning to pay for in the first place.

I know. Easier said than done.

Chapter 2

Love Is a Battlefield

~~Lessons~~ Scars from Adult Dating

*There are far, far better things ahead
than any we leave behind.*

—C. S. Lewis,
Collected Letters of C. S. Lewis

Name: Jody
Age: 30
Occupation: Elementary school teacher
City: La Habra, California

— — —

Hello,

"Unlucky in love." I always hated that phrase and never understood it. I never ever thought it would describe me. I grew up with the (wonderful fantasy/for sure to happen) dream that at age twenty-five I would be married, and by thirty I would own a home filled with three cute kids. Instead, I rent a modest one-bedroom apartment that I can barely afford, and not a single man is knocking on my front door, let alone texting, calling, emailing, or messaging me.

I was shy in high school, and dated a little in college. I met the "man of my dreams" once I was established in a career. After four years of my first true love relationship leading to nowhere, I broke it off. Even though it was my decision, I mourned that loss for more than a year and a half, and on December 31, 2010, I felt for the first time what real, true, bitter, heartwrenching rejection feels like.

The year 2011 was a blur, and in 2012 I got back up on the horse. I tend to go all in and am a huge believer in New Year's resolutions. Mine was to put myself out there no matter how uncomfortable I felt. So I let my friends set me up. I joined an online dating website. I became an avid member of a young adults' group in my church. I attended Sunday church service early and stayed after to mingle. I smiled at men in public, even if we were in a long line together at Starbucks and I had no witty words to say. I flirted in the sushi bar even in my workout clothes. Putting yourself out there works!

My particular problem has never been getting asked out but rather getting that second or third date, or better yet, the "relationship talk." None of the guys I met that year worked out. Putting myself out there in 2012 turned my Year of Revival into my Year of Rejection. What was I missing?

Now, even as I write to you, I am flooded with thoughts of what God wants me to do, what my next move should be, what my parents, family, and friends think is best. It's all too much to think about. I choose to stick with the only source of wisdom that transcends this world and its problems: "We must pay the most careful attention, therefore, to what we have heard, so that we do not drift away" (Heb. 2:1).

This nautical analogy in Hebrews calls to mind a picture of Jesus being our focus as we fight against the tide and waves, looking solely to him. The minute we stop putting him in focus, our boats drift. We feel lost and the memories of rejection take over.

I would like to tell you to never give up, feel lucky in love, and put yourself out there. I know that's hard to do, and there's no guarantee it will work out how you want it to. Instead, I will leave you with a challenge to fight and not drift away.

Love,

Jody

He showed me a ring.

It wasn't the right size, and he didn't pay for it, but I went along with it anyway.

As we stood in his parents' lakehouse, staring at the sparkling family heirloom he wanted to make mine, Jake and I talked excitedly about getting married and sharing our lives together. I couldn't believe it was all actually happening.

We'd met at church the previous summer. He asked me out on a date after a pool party one evening. I was hesitant to say yes, since I knew he was a couple of years younger than me (turned out to be three), but decided what the heck. We went for tacos by the beach and walked the pier the next weekend.

Pleasantly, the whole night turned out far better than I'd expected. He was a great listener, had a good sense of humor, and paid attention to things in my life other dates had breezed over. There was an instant ease to being with him that I had never felt before on a first date.

He was wearing a women's top. That was rough.

Okay, it wasn't really a women's top, but it was this navy blue ribbed shirt that I just couldn't really understand. I let it slide because it's important to let those things slide.

Plus his green eyes and broad shoulders made up for it.

After our second date, he told me he really liked me and wanted to date. With a deer—in—the—headlights expression, I said, "Thank you."

Not exactly smooth, but I wasn't used to a guy being so clear with me. I really liked it and ended the conversation with, "I'd like to keep getting to know you."

We dated the next few months and became exclusive on my twenty-eighth birthday. That October, we flew out to meet his family in Michigan, and in November I brought him to my family's Thanksgiving. I had never done that before, and aside from his showing up in a white version of the ribbed top (not kidding), it went perfectly.

With each milestone, Jake took the lead in our relation-ship and had total confidence in us. I started to notice he wasn't quite as secure in other areas of his life. His career, his relationships with his parents and friends, and his faith were constantly shifting. It concerned me a little, but he always said I was the one thing he was sure of. I knew that as long as that was true, we could figure out the other pieces together.

As I looked down at the ring, wedged awkwardly above my knuckle, memories of the globe he gave me so I could travel the world and of the time he told his mom he wished he'd never kissed another girl before me flooded in. The time he danced for hours like a crazy person at his cousin's wedding and the time he saved the bottle of wine we shared on our first Valentine's Day came rushing back. I thought of all the big and little ways I'd let him into my life—vacation with my family, sitting together at church, and cooking together—all the experiences that made me feel closer to him than to anyone else. I knew our differences could balance each other. He was the emotional, impulsive, and openhearted one. I was the realistic overthinker. Together, we could be a great team. I had finally found my someone.

We went home and started dreaming of where to have a reception, whom to have in the wedding party, and where to honeymoon. We both were elated.

For a time.

I can only guess that the weight of our ring conversation sank in, because unanswered phone calls, last-minute broken plans, and a cool shoulder made their way to me. I could feel him pulling away, so I tried to fix it by showing extra affection, planning his favorite outings, and talking more about our future. On my birthday, which he had gone all out for the year before, an Amazon.com package showed up at my house. No card. No wrapping paper. Just a book from his favorite series and a follow-up "happy birthday" text. I knew it was over.

When we finally had our "talk," he cried, apologized, said he'd changed his mind about me. He said he didn't know what he was doing with his life and that he couldn't be the guy I deserved. It was devastating. I was so confused as to how he could show me a ring and tell me he loved me, only to change his mind weeks later. Why would he do that? Why would he say all those things to me if he wasn't sure?

I was a total wreck. We didn't talk for what felt like a million years, but was only three days, before he came back apologizing. He said he had jumped the gun and wanted to get back together. Still numb from the breakup and tired of crying, I agreed.

He changed his mind again the next month.

Truthfully, I thought a mixture of good upbringing, self-preservation, and recreational romance-fiction reading would prepare me for anything. I'm not sure whether anyone ever tried to tell me what a broken heart feels like; if they did, I certainly wasn't paying any attention. I was completely unprepared for my breakup with Jake.

I was a hot mess with no clue how to get through it.

If you've been there, you'll remember all too well our unwanted friends named

Shock	Loss	Loneliness
Rejection	Death	Hopelessness
Anger	Bitterness	Fatigue
Embarrassment	Foolishness	Weakness
Failure	Betrayal	Fear

Just to name a few.

As I said, I never expected to experience a broken heart. I waited till I was ready to date the right guy. I was careful. I played my cards right. I had high standards. I truly believed my first all-in relationship would work out.

Over the next few months, I'd wake up in the morning, still half asleep, and forget for a moment that we had broken up. For a couple of short seconds, I'd experience the sweet relief of not being in a breakup. The weight on my chest and in the pit in my stomach were lifted and I'd almost smile.

Then I'd remember.

No.

No. We aren't together.

I'd have the pleasure of experiencing the breakup all over again. What a way to start the day.

God,

Where are you in this? You saw the part where I got dumped, right? Or is that kind of thing too small to be on your radar? Are breakups beneath you? A broken marriage, the death of a loved one—those we can talk about. But a broken heart— does it even matter to you?

It feels really awful. I'm hopeless and alone in this, and I'd like to believe you don't want me here. Deep down I worry you're waiting for me to just get over it already, so I can get back to caring about more important things.

That's the thing, God. I can't seem to fix my mind on anything else right now. It's all I think about. I've never felt so broken or afraid of what is next. I feel crazy even saying that. Help, please.

Cindy

It Takes Time

Getting over a broken heart takes time. Bottom line. I'm learning there are no shortcuts or skipping steps. It's just a crappy one-day-at-a-time kind of thing. We have to cycle through the stages of grief with each breakup:

Denial: "We're getting back together. This isn't over."

Bargaining: "God, if you give me one more chance, I'll

do [blank]." Or, "If only he'd realize [blank], then we'd be perfect for each other."

Anger: "He'll be sorry! I pity the next girl who has to put up with his crap."

Depression: Mascara tears, cookie dough consumed with wine, messy hair, and sweatshirts—lots of sweatshirt time.

Acceptance: "I'm better off without him. Or at least I will be one day."

Unfortunately, no one I know ever cycles through the stages nicely or neatly. It's usually two steps forward and one step back:

"Yay! I haven't texted him or stalked his Facebook in a week!"

"Boo! Found out he danced with some other girl at a wedding."

"Yay! Some friend's sister-in-law knows a guy from church who is single and may want to hang out."

"Boo! I need a sweatshirt and the only clean one I can find is his stupid college one."

We just have to ride these things out. Hour-by-hour in the beginning, day-by-day, and eventually a week goes by without a breakdown. At some point, you come out of the fog.

Life moves on—unless we choose to drag it out. Little temptresses like texting him at night and saying yes when he asks you to hang out seem like good ideas at the time. Trust me, I've done them all. I'm a repeat offender. It never went well in the end.

I learned the hard way that when you break up, it's best to cut it off completely. Don't see him or his friends, and don't keep your relationship memorabilia. Get rid of it. Move forward. Since there is no avoiding the process of getting over someone, it's up to you when you choose to start and how long you waste in the in-between.

In my experience, a broken heart is the devil's playground. I was susceptible to believing all kinds of lies during my breakup. Messages like, "I just wasn't good enough," or, "If only I'd tried harder or been like some other girl, *then* things would've turned out differently," all sounded totally reasonable. "No one else will want me, and even if someone else does, I won't truly be happy with anyone but my ex," and a million other false thoughts took root.

The most helpful thing I found during this time was to attempt to think about the truth whenever I could. It's hard not to obsess about the relationship. We are human. But whenever possible, I tried to focus on the fact that God loves me and wants the very best for me. Even if I didn't quite believe it yet, I told myself Jake was not God's best for me.

My friend Laura called from Tennessee one day to check in. I'll never forget her words: "Cindy, God isn't gonna give you up to just anybody."

Laura's message stuck. God cherishes me. He's protecting me. I'm his daughter, and he's not going to give me up to just any guy. He'll try to stop me from giving my heart to someone who isn't right for the job. In this crazy heartache, God's on my side. A broken heart is not too small for him to care about.

I once heard a pastor say that God keeps all our tears in a

jar. Of course, I didn't actually believe him, figuring it was some cheesy line he'd read on a religious sympathy card. Naturally, I went home and looked it up. Sure enough, right there in Psalm 56:8 (NASB) it says,

> You have taken account of my wanderings;
> Put my tears in Your bottle.
> Are they not in Your book?

I couldn't believe that God, with all he has going on, would take time to bottle up my tears. People bottle up important things. The tears I thought I cried all alone, the ones I thought were ridiculous and wasted on some boy, meant something to God. He not only saw them; he recorded and saved them, as if they mattered to him as much as they mattered to me. He sees all the boys and the breakups and the disappointing dates. And he cares about all of it.

Chapter 3

Call It What It Is

Why Being Single Is Lame

The only thing worse than a smug married couple;
lots of smug married couples.

—Bridget Jones,
Bridget Jones's Diary

Name: CJ
Age: 30
Occupation: Church office manager
City: Los Angeles

- - -

Dear sister,

If you had asked me ten years ago whether I thought I would still be single and inexperienced in romantic relationships at age thirty, I probably would have laughed in your face. That doesn't change the fact that I am both of those things.

My romantic history is sparse at best. I never had a boyfriend in high school and was only asked to the senior prom because my friend told my date that I really wanted to go with him and he was too sweet not to ask. The pattern continued in college, but I wasn't all that surprised because the guys on my secular and liberal campus were there to sleep with as many girls as possible, not lock one down for the rest of their lives. However, it was here that I started to make close friendships with guys that I hoped would eventually turn into romantic relationships, but never did. I put myself out there and formed relationships with multiple guys only to never leave the friend zone and eventually be overlooked when they moved on to find actual girlfriends. This began an unhealthy pattern I carried well into adulthood.

Then I found the guy who finally brought this seemingly endless cycle to a halt. I met Andrew at my part-time job as a waitress. (Girls, don't date waiters. They are bad news. Always.) We worked together for six months and had a casual friendship that sometimes included a quick beer after our closing shift on Friday nights. Right around this time a close girlfriend of mine was trying to get me out of my perpetual friend-zone status and agreed that it would probably be best if I didn't spend any more time investing in guys who didn't make it clear that their intent was to date. I thought the timing was perfect because Andrew suddenly started asking me to spend time with him outside of work. He called often, usually making plans to do very datelike things. I'm talking everything from dinner and a movie to day trips to San Diego. I just knew this was going to turn into something and decided to be patient and wait till he felt comfortable enough to tell me how he felt. I passively let six more months go by, and when we finally talked, the only thing he had to say was that he was moving back to his hometown in Texas.

This was a major blow to my self-esteem. I feel like I'm pretty average. I realize I don't look like a model, but I'm comfortable in my own skin and I hope that someone will find that attractive. I'm confident in my personality. I'm funny, low maintenance, and laid back, which I'm hoping is the trifecta to guys. But in the wake of Andrew, I felt like none of these things. I was my best self when I was with him, and that still wasn't enough.

The Andrew ordeal also made me question whether God really even cares to fill one of my heart's deepest desires. I (and most of my married girlfriends) have prayed for years that I would meet someone special, and it still hasn't happened. I know God's timing is perfect, but that's hard to hear when you feel like your prayers go unanswered.

A few weeks after Andrew left, I came across an underlined section in my Bible that seemed like the perfect response to the feelings I was working through. It's Daniel 3:18—the story of Shadrach, Meshach, and Abednego. Just as they are about to get thrown into the furnace, they tell King Nebuchadnezzar that their God will save them, "but even if he does not," they still refuse to worship the king's idol. For some reason that phrase stuck with me. Even if God doesn't send Mr. Right when or how I want, I still need to trust him and his timing and his genuine goodness.

Trust me, I wish there were a happy ending to this saga, but the truth is, I have been on two real dates in my entire life and my first kiss was on my twenty-second birthday. Somewhere along the way (probably around the eighth "friend" who didn't want to date me) I realized that doesn't mean something is wrong with me. Sure, my situation is uncommon, but that doesn't mean *I'm* not normal! Now I'm almost proud to tell people my story, which is part of why I'm writing it now.

Although my circumstances are unique to me, I hope my story gives encouragement to any other women fighting on the battlefield of love.

Your friend,

CJ

I realized that Christian girls age in dog years when my dad sat across the table from me at the coffee shop one morning.

Dad (hesitantly): "Cindy, I'm not worried, but—well, your mom, she is a little worried ... Basically, we just want to know if you are feeling called to the single life."

Me: "What the heck, Dad?! Single life is for freaks!" (A statement I'd now like to take back.)

Dad: "No. Apostle Paul was called to the single life."

Me (shrieking): "Dad! Paul was a freak! I'm pretty sure the Bible actually says that somewhere."

Dad: "Either way, honey, we know your breakup with Jake was tough. We just want you to know it is okay to be single as long as you need to. We love you and are proud of you no matter what. Your mom and I would be okay if you aren't feeling like marriage is something you want."

Me: "Okay, um, thanks ... can we please just let this go?"

Called to the single life? Of course I want to get married some-day! I thought on the way to the car. *I don't blow-dry my hair for kicks.* What hadn't occurred to me till right then was that people in my life were worried about it. Apparently I had officially crossed over into some other group where people wondered why you weren't married yet.

"Yet."

Can we just all agree never to use that word?

It implies a silent shift has taken place, somewhere between the ages of twenty-eight and twenty-nine, where you go from "fun and normal girl with lots of single friends" to "awkward, tragically still-single girl who has no more age-appropriate friends to play with."

In my attempt to get back on track, I started ring-checking and tallying the shrinking number of other singles at my get-togethers with friends. Even I had to admit there weren't many left. *Have I missed the boat? I didn't even know there was a boat! Where did everyone get on this boat?!*

After a certain point, if your primary social network is Christian, being a single female is perceived as a problem. People say things like, "Don't worry! It will be your turn soon!" or, "My husband and I think you're great! We just can't figure out why you're still single and we pray for your partner all the time." I think it's the prayers that make you feel like you've just been diagnosed with an illness that needs to be cured immediately. Yep, it's me and my singleness on the prayer chain this week, right next to Ethel and her upcoming hip replacement surgery.

Great.

And while I don't think singleness should be seen as a problem, I have to admit there are some challenging parts that can easily get the best of us.

Holidays

I'm convinced that holidays are designed for the enjoyment of kids and couples. It's more of a slow and steady torture for us singles. We are forced to endure Thanksgiving at the kid's table and boring Christmas parties where the main topics of conversation are breastfeeding, tummy time, and which minivan gets the best mileage. We have no one to kiss at New Year's. Or we kiss some random guy, and then our married friends get all judgey about it. *Really? You can't cut me some slack here? I did just pretend to act surprised when your two-year-old liked the box his toy came in at Christmas.*

"Can you believe that?" his mom said with huge, dumb eyes.

"Oh yeah, hysterical. So cute," I kindly replied while wondering whether 11:30 a.m. was too early to spike the eggnog.

The number one reason I find myself jealous of married people this time of year is because they get to choose which functions they attend and which ones they will oh-so conveniently be at their spouse's family for.

Nice move, married people. Nice move.

Don't worry about me. I'm trapped cherishing this opportunity to awkwardly navigate the room looking for someone to sit by. A quick survey usually tells me I'll be stuck talking to your small group leader's wife about how *For Women Only* changed her marriage. Unless, of course, I prefer cozying up to the older skeezy guy wearing a Hawaiian shirt hogging all the spinach dip. *Thanks, by the way, for inviting him for me. I really appreciate it. This is a total upgrade from last year, when everyone got to watch your neighbor flirt with me using actual card tricks.*

Every year, I start the holiday season off optimistic. I tell myself it's going to be a good one. Somewhere between Thanksgiving and Christmas Day, I've used up all my charm and earned the Worst Most Scroogiest Family Member/Terrible Friend/Who Invited Her? award. Usually after snapping at a distant relative's well-intentioned question about my dating life. You know when you bite the inside of your mouth and it swells? So you accidentally keep biting it? The continuous string of holiday festivities is like that. It's a vicious cycle.

Time Crunch

Singles simply can't win in the time management department. My best advice here is just to get used to disappointing people. The sooner you come to terms with this, the better. Expect your married friends to think you have all the time in the world. Most of them will never notice that everyone else in your life feels entitled to you too. All of the time.

If you've ever stared frightfully at your overcommitted calendar and found nothing but volunteer training meetings, work trips, your cousin's high school band recital, and three baby showers (why must these take seven hours and leave you feeling hungover?), then you know what I'm talking about. Somehow, because you are single, you are supposed to fit what you have to do around what everyone else has going on. And still be available to meet a guy.

Why wouldn't you have time to drive during rush hour all the way to a stay-at-home mom friend's house after work? Why would you turn down leading a small group, greeting on Sunday, or volunteering in the nursery? It's not as if you have a family to tend to.

Forget leaving anything early or showing up late. Unlike

a married person, who can go home for her husband's epic—
yet daily—arrival home from work, you must stay till the
end. Or do as I do—opt for the sneak-away and hope they
don't notice.

Wedding Season

Standing there wearing my first wedding dress (made of toi-
let paper, incidentally), I realized I was in a hostile environment. If I made it past hours of polite conversation with my
friend's future mother-in-law's coworker, I still had to smile
through multiple "When is it your turn?" and "I think you're
next!" comments before they'd let me leave.

In one summer, I attended seven weddings, two one-year-
olds' birthday parties, two graduation parties, a bachelorette
weekend, a baby shower, and six bridal showers. Colorful,
oddly shaped envelopes kept piling up, inviting me to cel-
ebrate other people's lives with money I didn't have. Dazed,
I pictured girls standing around talking endlessly about hot
topics like cabinetry and photographers. I phoned my mom
to swear about the horrific cost of bridesmaid's dresses and
shower gifts. She hates it when I swear.

Clearly my friend's events are not about me, and I would
never want them to be. I dearly love the girls in my life and
would never actually miss their celebrations. But here, with
you, can I just tell it like it is? Can I be honest about the fact
that I want to go to these events but I don't always like them?
Is it possible to be happy for someone I love while admitting
it's hard? Especially when you're fresh out of a breakup or a

string of bad first dates, attending weddings alone and being the last single friend at a shower sucks. It just does.

Lately, I've been trying to go easy on myself. Part of growing up is understanding you can't please everyone. For example, I don't take expensive gifts to every event anymore. I grew tired of saving and spending my small paycheck on someone else's life. I figure any friends who can't understand a budget and who need a Williams Sonoma panini press as part of the deal probably won't be lifelong friends anyway. Unless I get married. In which case, let's keep this thing going. And I want a panini press.

I've started saying no to things, and I never stay till the end if I don't want to. I'm hoping time spent at social gatherings is about quality, not quantity. Knowing I'm not trapped somewhere helps me be a semidecent person at awkward functions. (Emphasis on semi.)

Finally, I've decided what kind of friend I want to be. I want to be a good single friend to my married friends regardless of how I'm feeling at the moment. While I'm not promising I won't dance away from the mom group at their bachelorette parties or zone out while they open dish towels at their showers, I am trying. I am committed to doing what it takes to maintain the friendship even though we are in different stages.

There is no excuse for showing up as a bitter downer. No one likes that girl anyway. My friends can still count on me to bring critical mass to the dance floor, hold their dresses while they pee, and cry real love tears during the speeches. However, I do plan on being conveniently busy during the bouquet toss.

Summer Budget

Event	$$ Money $$	Life Points
7 weddings	−$45 × 3 for gifts −$940 maid of honor ☹ −$325 for bridesmaid's dresses	+ 3 ugly bridesmaid dresses −7 good beach days missed ☹ −1 good dress cute guy spilled wine on + 1 follow-up date (ended lame) + 4 lbs. of wedding cake
2 first b-day parties	Forget it ...	+ 1 cute uncle at the party ☺
6 bridal showers	−$15 Went in on a group gift! Score! −$45 × 4 for gifts $0 Mom paid for gift!	−1 million weekend hours! + 14 Advil + 2 shower prizes. I am good at shower games!
1 baby shower	−$35 Bought cutest baby dress and shoes!	−1 tank of gas b/c shower was 1,000 miles away in suburbia
1 bachelorette weekend	Is it bad I didn't keep track? #Imbrokeanyway	+ 1 awesome weekend! + 7 good Facebook pics

Being No One's Someone

Jody (sobbing on the phone): "Cin?"

Me: "Jody? Hey. Are you okay?"

Jody: "Yes ... I just, I just hate this! I thought I was doing better about Steven [loser ex-boyfriend, dated three years], but ... *sniff, sniff* ... I need a ride from the airport and *he* used to always take me and now he can't take me and I just ... I don't know who to call now."

There are a lot of big and little things that are hard about being single. For me, the biggest is being no one's someone.

Was it okay for Jody to call me for a ride? Absolutely. Could she have called her mom? Of course. But this sort of thing just makes you feel like you're back in high school and solidifies that you still don't have your life together. Getting a ride from the airport is a job for the person you are with, the person on your emergency and W-4 forms. Going through your phone, trying to remember who you inconvenienced last time, reminds you that you don't have that significant person on speed dial.

As I get older, I'm increasingly dependent on people who are no longer depending on me, and it's hard. It's vulnerable needing someone who doesn't really need me. It's tough admitting I put things on friends, family members, and random checkout ladies at the grocery store that they weren't designed to carry. Dates to boring office parties, consoling sob fests, and listening to mindless chatter about the girl from work's crappy boyfriend are all meant for the kind of relationship you and I don't have.

Have you ever found yourself telling ten different people everything that happened to you over the weekend and wondering when you became such a blabbermouth? It's embarrassing, but it's not your fault. I believe you were made to have someone who makes you feel heard in one shot. Are you tired of dreading celebrations you should be looking forward to? It's lonely, and you aren't the only girl who feels this way. Does your dad or male coworker still have to bail you out of a flat tire? It stinks, but it doesn't mean there is something wrong with you.

There is nothing wrong with you.

Don't let anyone make you feel like there is.

- -

A Note to Married People
What Not to Say to Your Single Friends

Hello!

If you are reading this, there is a good chance you are married and friends with a single girl. (She may have passed this list your way.) Basically, I'm going to spell out all the things she wishes she could say to you but is too worried about hurting your feelings. I emailed my single friends to help compile a list of what really gets under our skin, at best, and sends us into the bathroom at couples' parties crying, at worst.

Please feel free to both take my advice and be really, really annoyed with me.

XOXO,

Cindy

1. Don't talk crap on your single friends' exes. Here's the deal: We loved them. Even when they were terrible guys. Just like you love your husband, the guy we would never talk bad about even when he messes up. There is a time and place for your real opinion. We'll let you know when that is.

2. Don't tell your single friends it's about being content. Most of the world gets married. You got married. Especially in Christian American circles, marriage starts fairly young and as hard as it is to go without it at times, it's much worse when someone makes you feel guilty for wanting it.

Please be careful not to imply that we should feel content with God either. All we take away is that in addition to being single, we are also doing a terrible job following Jesus. There is room in the Christian life to be sad. There is room to be frustrated. We are often so quick to rush people into being okay that we make them feel it's wrong to be anything short of content.

3. Don't compare your single friends' adult relationships to your high school or college ones. We understand you dated him for four-plus years. We're sure it was meaningful. No one is saying it's not. But adult relationships and teenage ones are different ball games. Adult relationships typically start out on a serious foot. If we break up, it isn't just about taking down a few sorority dance pictures; we are breaking up with an entire future. The wedding, the house, and the growing old together that we most likely talked about with our ex will never come to pass. Nearly every friend I've walked through an adult breakup with has turned to me at some point and said, "I feel like I'm going through a divorce."

4. Please don't complain in front of your single friends about having to have sex with your husband. Save that for your married friends. One friend wrote, "If you want to have an honest conversation about how your expectations for sex have changed, by all means, share. We absolutely care about that. But don't make flippant comments on how put out you are by your active sex life. Some of us are holding on by the skin of our teeth here!"

5. Don't call your single friends at 10:00 a.m. and ask them if they're awake yet. We're single, not children. Please don't forget to ask us for advice on finances or business. We still have life experience outside of relationship experience.

Also, don't always give us the back seat or the pullout couch on vacation while the marrieds take the beds. We all like a good mattress. And you know it.

6. Remember that you don't understand what it's like to be alone at this age. If we come to you hurting, venting, or complaining, please don't find a way to work in the fact that you think we should be happy. (Unless we've done it a hundred times and need to snap out of it. We need a good kick every once in awhile too.) Doing everything by ourselves that we thought we'd do with a spouse can be rough at times.

A lady at my church asked me once if she could pray for me. I had just ended my relationship with Jake and quit my job (because I thought I would be moving to where he was). I tried to explain to her that I had no idea how to rebuild my life at this point. I had no direction and no one to tie me down somewhere. She listened and began her prayer this way: "Lord, please help Cindy to see the beauty in her opportunity and independence. Help her to see that people would kill for her freedom and to be thankful."

At that time, I'd had enough freedom. I wanted to settle down with someone. Being single doesn't always feel like opportunity. Some days it feels like being lost and behind. Even with a full social life of friends and family, the truth is we eat most meals alone. We drive alone, come home to an empty house, and put our suitcases in the overhead storage compartment all by ourselves. If you're married, you most likely don't live that way.

I know there are busy moms who would kill for some alone time. There are married people who would love the luxury of a trip with girlfirends. I get (in theory) that having kids and a spouse is stressful, hard work, and a ton of responsibility. It's probably good and bad depending on the day. The same goes for being single. It isn't perfect on either side.

7. Don't set two single Christian friends up just because they are both Christian. If our only common denominators are single and religion, stop yourself. Please use some judgment when orchestrating these setups.

8. Don't forget to set your single friends up. Married friends will often say, "I know someone you have to meet! You would be perfect together." And then that's the last anyone ever hears of it. Don't be fooled; we are totally reliant on you to get that ball rolling. Make the phone call, organize the BBQ, send them the number! If it's someone you truly think is a good fit, we'll be grateful. And even toast you at the wedding . . . *if* you actually come through.

9a. Don't make your single friends' love life, or lack thereof, the most pressing thing to inquire about every time you see them. (As though everything else in our lives is subpar.) One friend wrote, "I often get random, little encouraging cards from my married friends saying, 'I don't know why you haven't found someone, but know that I'm praying for Mr. Right to come soon.' I don't really appreciate this. I mean, thank you for praying, but I'm also concerned with finding a career, mentoring high school girls, and navigating healthy relationships with my crazy retired parents who may kill each other if I don't check in on them every week! Since you're already praying, could you add those to the top of the list?"

When our married friends make our dating lives the center

of attention, we sense pity. We wonder why the other parts of our lives don't matter as much as this one area we can't control. I imagine it would feel the same if we asked only about your baby and never about you. Yes, the baby is taking up most of your attention, but you are still valuable in other ways.

9b. Don't ask your single friends for detailed updates about their relationships and not be honest about your marriage. For some reason, everyone and their mother feels they can ask about my dating life. If I have a boyfriend at the time, they immediately want to know how it's going and when we are getting married. Look, if I'm not telling you I'm engaged, it's probably something he and I are carefully sorting through. I'd prefer not to go around blabbing about it. And unfortunately it would be wildly inappropriate for me to return the inquiry with, "How's your marriage going?" I may as well ask, "How are your finances? How's your diet? How often are you two having sex?" Off limits.

Sharing details communicates a level of friendship and trust. With our close married friends, single people want to be confided in with equal vulnerability. If you aren't going to ante up, don't ask us to just so you can be in the loop or give us your two cents. I've had conversations that look like this:

Married friend presses for details.
I provide details.
Married friend gives advice.
I listen and try to think of how to explain my side without being rude.
Married friend continues with advice.

I'm quiet and hopefully polite.

Conversation ends.

Whether they've been married exactly thirteen days or this is their first serious relationship and my fifth, I'm always the student in the situation. It's not a great climate for growing a friendship, as you can imagine.

10. Don't count your single friends out as aunties! We may not have the baby skills on lockdown, but we do care. We do want to be at important milestones, buy baby clothes, and one day tell your kids college stories about you that you'd prefer we didn't share. We do want to have dinner at your house with the family (and then grab a drink after you put them to bed).

11. Don't assume every single person is looking for a relationship. I would argue that deep down, 97 percent are looking. (This is not a real statistic; I completely made it up on my own.) Still, the 3 percent who don't want a relationship do matter, and it's important to know where a friend stands. Don't be quick to put your expectations on them.

Equally as important: don't assume someone who wants to get married someday is *always* looking. I've gone through several phases in my adult singleness. There are times I really want to meet someone and times I'm very glad to be on my own. There are seasons when I'm open to dating and seasons when I say no because I'm excited about investing in other things. It's best to ask where we are as opposed to jumping to your own conclusion.

A friend of mine wrote this, "Since I'm at a supercontent phase, I don't like people assuming I want to be set up. Some of my coworkers said yesterday, 'Oh, you're single; we're looking for the perfect man for you!' Meanwhile, I'm looking for the perfect sewing machine and yoga class and maybe a new church; I am *not* looking for a man. If I happen upon a man on my way to yoga and he's not an idiot, I may stop and talk to him, but I'm for sure not going there to look."

In summation, all people, married and single, want to feel like their stage of life is okay. We all want to feel like we are on the right track. It can hurt to feel like everyone is waiting, prodding, expecting, or feeling bad about the way your life is going. This tends to come out in the way we talk to each other. It's important for both sides to listen and to kindly choose our words carefully.

I really hope my *own* married friends don't think this section is all about things they've done, because it is not. Please still talk to me. ☺

- -

Chapter 4

Their Gain Is Your Loss

When Your Friends Get Engaged

"A…a what kind of friend?"
"A bosom friend—an intimate friend, you know—
a really kindred spirit to whom I can confide my inmost soul.
I've dreamed of meeting her all my life."

—Anne Shirley,
in *Anne of Green Gables*

Name: Laura
Age: 26
Occupation: Speech-language pathologist
City: Dyersburg, Tennessee (middle of nowhere, USA)

‑ ‑ ‑

Dear sister,

My name is Laura, and I would say I'm a normal, southern girl. I'd like to think of myself as smart, kindhearted, easily amused, and one who loves to dance, go to sporting events, and watch movies. I grew up, and currently live, in a small farm town, but I have moved around to several different places in the South and along the West Coast (where I met Cindy!) and have traveled quite a bit. Because of that, I've seen many different cultures and dated guys of all walks of life. ☺ My point is this: I'm not a freak. I'm a small-town girl with big-city dreams. Nothing special, nothing weird. I'm normal.

As for my love life: what a rollercoaster. I wouldn't be able to count the number of guys I've dated. I don't say that braggingly—I say that because not one of them worked out. After analysis, I realized my love life was a continuous cycle—never being broken.

This is how it went:

I would date a guy for a short amount of time, become infatuated, fall in love, and practically be married in my mind within a few months. But I would never let *him* know. I always tried to play the cool card. Never nagged. Never controlled. Never complained. Always positive. Always easygoing. Always having a good time. He would take me to meet his parents, take me on vacations, and tell me I was the girl of his dreams. Then one day, it would all stop. Phone calls would be sporadic, interest was less. This has happened multiple times, girls—not just once.

So naturally, I would think every single time, *What is wrong with me? What did I do? Why does this keep happening?* I would analyze every single conversation and every move I made from start to finish of the relationship until I was blue in the face and sick to my stomach. There were never any answers. He was just not that into me, even though he said he was.

After that relationship, I would date a safe guy, one who wasn't really a thrill. I didn't get butterflies and was never really attracted to him physically. I wanted so desperately to like him because I knew he wouldn't hurt me like the others. He was kind, gentle, consistent, and adored me. What more could a girl want? I would feel shame and guilt for not liking him back. "God, help me to like this one—he's good!" I would try it for a few weeks, giving myself some time to fall for him, but it would never happen. So then back to the "wild card" boy I would go. And the cycle continued.

Everyone would say the same thing: "It's all part of God's plan. It's his will." Yeah, yeah, yeah. I get it. I'm supposed to say that and feel that way. Then one day, it finally clicked, but in a different way. I finally realized, *I'm the prize*. God sees *me* as the prize. I'm not doing anything wrong with these boys. God puts them in my life to both strengthen and soften my heart. He then removes them for my own good. He has control, and he is removing these boys from my life because *they* aren't right for *me*. These boys aren't rejecting me. *God* is rejecting these boys *for me*.

It suddenly made sense. All of those flaws from all of those boys that I tried to justify, cover up, and downright ignore before were shown to me in broad daylight. Hello! Those boys were not the ones for me. God cherishes my normal, southern, big-city-dreams heart, and he wants only the very best to handle it.

And the same goes for you. God, who holds the universe in his hands, holds your beautiful heart in his hands too. He will hand it over only to the utmost worthy man.

Love,

Laura

P.S. "But do not forget this one thing, dear friends: With the Lord a day is like a thousand years, and a thousand years are like a day. The Lord is not slow in keeping his promise, as some understand slowness" (2 Peter 3:8–9). He is not slow in action in fulfilling the desires of your heart. He is meticulous in his planning and preparation for your love and your life. He plans every detail for perfection, so be patient! He has much joy in store for you.

- -

I'll never forget the moment I found out my best friend was engaged. I was driving home from a coffee date with Jake. We weren't together at the time, so I shouldn't have been there in the first place. After a month of not communicating, he and I ran into each other outside of church and he asked if I wanted to grab lunch. Stupidly, I said yes. Lunch turned into coffee, which turned into dinner. On the drive home, while trying to decide if I was happy or angry with myself, the phone rang. Elise was getting married and wanted to know if I'd be her maid of honor.

When you find out another one of your friends is engaged, there is this moment when your legs stiffen and a slight panic runs through your veins. You hear your heart pounding in your ears. Your brain knows this is the wrong response and warns you that your emotion toward the "good" news is not only selfish but also wildly inappropriate. Thankfully, your mother's voice in your head saves you from making a fool of yourself, and you remember to force the corners of your mouth into a smile. This particular form of grin does not include your eyes, because, well, that would take an act of God or true joy, neither of which is bailing you out at this moment.

You are not a hundred percent excited about your friend's engagement.

You are not allowed to say this.

After the initial shock, you enter phase two. You must come to terms with your selfish attitude. Doused in guilt, you think, *Wow, am I really that awful of a human being that I can't be happy for someone I love?*

You attempt to figure out what is going on with you. *Why all the ugliness? I knew this day was coming. I love my friend. I'm happy for her. Why am I being like this?*

Most would quickly attribute the unpleasant dark side to one thing: jealousy.

While there is some of that going on, I don't think it's that simple. It isn't just about jealousy. Envy makes up a percentage of the bad feeling, but it is not fully to blame. We don't actually want our friends' husbands, relationships, or even their timing. (Okay, maybe the timing.) So, what then? Why the bad feelings?

I believe the dominant emotion you and I feel when a friend moves on to marriage is loss. It's the end of an era. It's the closing of a chapter. It's a pain—new roommate to find, new confidant to acquire, and lots and lots of parties coming your way while you sort this all out. In a sense, a friend's getting engaged is a form of "you and I aren't working out anymore, and I've found someone new." You've been dumped. Suddenly, the good days are over and your friend has moved on to greener pastures. You, of course, haven't, and will now be spending your nights alone. Your shopping buddy, roommate, travel partner, bar wingman, first date outfit judger, single commiserator is gone. You were single before she left; you weren't alone until she got engaged.

And while there are plenty of places for a gal to cry over

a boyfriend breakup, you can't show that you are upset when a friend gets married. Rather than being excused by society to sulk in your room with wine and Netflix, it's time to buy a gift, host a shower, write a speech, and have a front row seat to a show titled "My Best Friend Has Found Love. I'm Probably Going to Die Alone. But Hey, at Least I Got a Bridesmaid's Dress."

What if I told you that the crappy, crazy feeling inside is totally legitimate? Not that acting out because of it is a good idea, but the painful emotion itself is normal. Friendship, it turns out, is a vital component of our emotional, spiritual, and even physical health. For women in particular, our bonds of friendship with our girlfriends are our lifelines. This form of relationship is our one shared universal relational experience. We don't all get married, know our parents, or have siblings. But we have all had a taste of friendship. Every culture and religion allows for friendship to happen. It is in our DNA to seek it out in some form.

For whatever reason, friendship takes a back seat to other relationships and is often seen as silly or trivial in the grand scheme of things. Even the phrase "girl time" implies it's a luxury of sorts, not a necessity. In the Christian world, you hear very little about the importance of friendship. We promote community, small groups, and accountability partners, but they are encouraged for a purpose—spiritual growth or church involvement—rather than as ends in and of themselves. Friendship isn't communicated as the underlying value.

Our friends are essential to our well-being, and this loss of companionship is a very large part of why we are often unhappy as singles. Getting married is an absolutely wonderful thing for your friend, but it doesn't negate the fact that it can bring on a huge loss for you.

Validation

Our single friends do more than keep us company; they affirm our way of life. Don't underestimate the power of validation. Most of us fail to realize that our desire to be married is more than wanting to find a husband. It isn't that we are desperate, romantic freaks, or lonely all the time. Part of why we want to meet someone is because we don't want to be the odd man out.

Picture this for a moment. All your friends are still single. You all share apartments, still get together for group outings where no one is paired off, plan group vacations, and so on. Now ask yourself, "How much do I feel the need to get married right now in this reality?" For me, the need is less. It turns out that I love a lot about my life; I simply want to enjoy it with my friends. You and I are not only looking for a romantic relationship; it's also friendship that we seek.

And it's friendship that we lose when our friends get married. Things can't go back to the way they were when we all were single, and it's not easy to replace close friends. After a certain age, we start to feel like we just keep gathering younger and younger friends. Suddenly, we are surrounded by people who don't know what *Saved by the Bell* is and want to stay out until three in the morning. These new friends don't fill the void as nicely as the people we grew up with in our twenties. In my experience, this loss adds fuel to the fiery lie that I've fallen behind.

Physical Survival

Friendship has profound effects on our bodies. According to the head of psychiatry at Stanford University, "One of the best things that a man can do for his health is to be married to a woman, whereas for a woman, one of the best things she can do for her health is to nurture her relationships with her girlfriends."[2] This finding has been medically supported on a number of occasions. A study out of the University of California by Dr. Laura Cousin Klein and Shelley Taylor found that emotionally connecting with other women lowers blood pressure, heart rate, and cholesterol. Similar studies have found that regular social connection improves a person's odds of beating cancer, heart disease, depression, and a slew of other illnesses. According to a Nurses' Health Study at Harvard, low levels of connection were determined to be equally as dangerous as smoking fifteen cigarettes and twice as harmful as obesity. Don't feel so bad about splurging at girls' night now, huh?

Our friend time is keeping us alive and healthy. Spending time with friends is as important as eating right, working out, and managing stress. It's only natural that our response to a friend's moving on is fear and pain. The news isn't good for us in this sense. We were designed to need this type of connection, and our perception is that an engagement has threatened it.

Emotional Survival

According to John Cacioppo, author of *Loneliness: Human Nature and the Need for Social Connection*, we need at least one or two close friends to ward off loneliness. The problem with loneliness is that it can sneak up on you. One night you feel like all is right in your social world, and the next thing you know, all your friends are married and have shiny new couple friends. Suddenly, you feel alone.

An interviewer once asked Mother Teresa to talk about the greatest pain she had ever witnessed. Rather than tell a story of disease, famine, or poverty, she said that loneliness was the greatest pain she'd seen. It is a powerful feeling, and in the context of friends getting married, most go straight to thinking we are lonely because we don't have a spouse. And while that can be part of it, the loss of a friend is also at play blame. It isn't just about being single.

Typically, when we are growing up, our parents and siblings are our primary relationships. As we reach adolescence, our friends often start moving up the ladder and stay toward the top until we get married and start families of our own. The reason it is painful when a friend moves on while you are single is that while she is still your number one, you are no longer hers. A shift has taken place in the prioritization of the relationship. While we may not be able to put our finger on it, we definitely feel it.

Hopefully we are on the same page in that spouse and kids should trump friends. However, this doesn't take away the effect the change has on your friendship. In 2012, the Barna Group conducted a fascinating study called *Christian Women Today*. In the section "A Look at Women's Lifestyles, Priorities, and Time Commitments," 53 percent of women said their family is their highest priority. The more shocking statistic is that only 3 percent of women said friendship is their top priority. If you are feeling less important to your married friends, it's because you *are* less important. Whether this is right or wrong, it hurts.

In addition to growing apart in importance, what you believe about your core identity is changing as well. In the same Barna study, 62 percent of women indicated that their most important role is as a mother. Thirteen percent marked follower of Jesus, and 11 percent marked wife. Only 3 percent identified their role as an employee as the most important, and only 2 percent marked their role as a friend as most important.

Barna didn't break this study down between marrieds and singles, but you can see how our identities would be flipped. Without a husband or a baby, our core identity roles — outside of our faith — are typically in our jobs and friendships. Bottom line, we feel differently about who we are fundamentally.

Until you and I are in the same boat as our married and mom friends, there is going to be some natural separation. Some married friends cross these lines better than others, just as some of us single folk navigate between them more seamlessly as well. At any rate, whether they know it or not, they need us as much as we need them. An Australian study conducted by the Center for Aging Studies discovered that "having a spouse, close relatives, or even lots of loving children had no impact on survival." After following fifteen hundred older people for ten years, they discovered that those with a large circle of friends outlived those with the fewest number of friends by 22 percent. Only a circle of friends raised the rate of survival.

Spiritual Survival

I believe that God not only gave us friendship as a gift but also hardwired us to depend on it. From the very beginning, God is seen as a relational God, enjoying the perfect relationship between Father, Son, and Holy Spirit. As the biblical story continues, God moves, acts, and restores through relationships. Many of the stories in Scripture play out through the context of friends: David and Jonathan, Ruth and Naomi, Jesus and his disciples, and Elizabeth and Mary, to name a few. The bonds of friendship are a foundational part of how the church was formed, is sustained, and moves forward. Similarly, it is this same bond that keeps our personal spiritual lives afloat. We need close friends if we are going to make it.

Underestimating the importance of true, deep, close friendship is partially the reason so many fall away from faith. We often miss its value and aren't sure how to nurture this form of relationship. I've sat through plenty of sermons on being good husbands, wives, parents, children, and employees, but rarely on being good friends.

I came across a quote by William Blake that describes our need for friendship:

I looked for my soul, but my soul I could not see.
I looked for my God, but my God eluded me.
I looked for a friend and then I found all three.

There are times when you and I just can't find ourselves. It is in these moments that our friends come alongside to remind us who we are. They are the ones who can see our worth when we no longer can. Most of us have walked

71

through dark times when God felt distant or even nonexistent. Our friends are meant to hang in there with us and point us to Jesus when we can't find him. They display his love when we no longer feel his presence and encourage us with truth and prayer. Our spiritual lives will not survive without our friends. While prayer, church, and Bible study are important to our spiritual growth, we need to be equally concerned with the health of our Christian friendships if we are going to thrive.

This type of friendship knows no relationship status. Your married friends need your spiritual friendship as much as you need theirs. Even with a husband, they still need you. We have to fight for these relationships, even as we ride out the changes.

As of today, I've lived with eight brides as they planned their weddings. I've been a bridesmaid sixteen times and a maid of honor twice. Some of those women were very close to me and caused great loss. When Elise got married, I was in a hard season. I thought that would be the summer I'd get married. I felt cheated and angry that God seemed to be rubbing my failed relationship in my face.

Instead, he was teaching me about the person I could be if I took my eyes off of myself and put them on him. I needed to move past my own sadness and be there for my friend. I think a good word for this is dignity.

Dignity goes against our culture's strong desire to always be real and authentic, because it means to act with excellence and self-worth at all times, regardless of the situation. What is interesting about this trait is that when you act with it, you bestow it on others. Had I behaved poorly at Elise's wedding, because I felt like it, I wouldn't have given proper dignity to my friend and to the importance of her special day.

Proverbs 31:25 speaks of a woman "clothed with strength and dignity, and she laughs without fear of the future" (NLT). If you read the whole chapter, you gather that this woman is in control of her actions and reactions. She moves with dignity because she has chosen to do so. "She laughs without fear of the future" because she trusts God will be with her tomorrow, and that trust has the final word, not her circumstances or emotions.

I'm not saying I got it right every time, but looking back, that wedding was the first time I practiced dignity. I asked God to help me behave outside of my frustrations. As I began, each smile and positive word felt forced and difficult. Slowly, as the wedding day came, my attitude began to change and my heart soon followed. In the end, Elise's wedding was one of the most beautiful days of my life. Watching her marry a good man gave me truly unexpected joy deep in my soul.

This awful feeling you are carrying around during this time of transition is far more than petty jealousy. You're responding to a very real and intense loss in your life, and it isn't easy to know what to do with that pain. Know that this grief may be the very thing that leads you to become a better you.

Chapter 5

I'm Single, Not Desperate

Why Being Single Is Awesome

Live, travel, adventure, bless, and don't be sorry.

—Jack Kerouac

Name: Brittany
Age: 31
Occupation: NBA advertisement
City: Los Angeles

— — —

Hello,

I had coffee with my ex-boyfriend this morning. In my opinion, he is one of the best catches on the planet. He is incredibly smart, fun, kind, successful, and the list can go on forever. We dated for four years and I would not take back one second of time with him. I ended the relationship because I did not want to marry him. If my goal in life had been to get married, then he would have been the perfect candidate. But my goal in life was not, and still is not, to get married. My goal is to find love and happiness and hopefully, somehow, share that with others. I have no interest in living my life according to what society says or what everyone else is doing. If I did, I would have missed out on traveling around the world, working for three professional sports teams, and, most important, meeting the person I do want to marry. He doesn't complete me, because I was complete before I met him, but he does make me better. We are better together, like the Jack Johnson song—and now I've gone and referenced the most popular wedding song of the twenty-first century after telling you that my goal in life is *not* to get married, so I'll get back on track with this.

I do not believe that anyone is better just because they are married or in a relationship. I don't look at my single friends and feel sorry for them. Instead, I think of how rich their lives are as they meet new people, take on hobbies, and enjoy wine and chocolate for dinner whenever they want and don't have to justify it to anyone. The biggest piece of advice that I can offer single women is to enjoy this time and be present in these moments. You can't get them back. A big bonus to this mindset is that when you are really happy and comfortable with who you are, people want to be around you, and that includes guys. My boyfriend is attracted to the fact that I am a secure woman who is with him not to be "in a relationship" but because we enhance and enrich each other's lives. I believe that the ability to love and be loved is the best gift we have on this earth and it is truly awesome to be in a great relationship. It is definitely okay to want that right person and partner in life, but it can also be wonderful to live a fulfilling single life. Whichever path you are on or go down, the important thing is to enjoy the ride along the way.

Sincerely,

Brittany

I'd love to tell you that the time in between my breakup with Jake and getting back on the dating horse was awesome. But that would be a lie. It was a bit of a nightmare. The way I saw it, I was turning thirty, was single, and my friends and family were all moving on while I stayed still. Stuck. Jake didn't love me, and I felt like God didn't care about what I wanted. Not one area of my life was going well. Nothing looked the way I wanted it to. All I wanted was to hit a restart button.

I was that girl, the girl who cried about her stupid ex-boyfriend in the break room next to the copier. The girl who might fall apart when a love song played on the radio. My boss kindly told me to take some time off. I needed to pull it together.

My parents were visiting my youngest brother, Matt, in Europe at the time, and I joined them last minute. I'm so thankful I did. Draining my savings account (plus a little help from good old Mom and Dad) was the best decision I'd made in a long time.

Seeing my family slowly and surely brought sunshine back into my life. We hiked, saw the sights, ate amazing food, and swam in the most beautiful water I'd ever seen. The world started to feel welcoming again.

Eventually, my family went home and I stayed in Barcelona by myself for a couple of days. There's something magical about exploring a city alone. It's easier to notice all the sights, sounds, and smells—all the windows into possible lives you don't have but could. It makes everything feel less dramatic back home. My world had felt so tiny—population 2: Jake and the mess he'd made—for too long. It was time to remember the world was still huge and filled with adventure and opportunity.

On my last night, I went to dinner with two guys from my hostel, an Australian and a Canadian, and their friend Isa, who was from Barcelona. Isa was twenty-nine, a med student, and beautiful inside and out. I could tell we would be good friends if we lived on the same continent.

At one point during the meal, she leaned over and asked why I was in Spain. I wasn't sure how to explain it all, especially in my limited Spanish, so I simply told her a guy back home had broken my heart. Her eyes told me she got it right away, and I'll never forget her response, "No hay mal que cien años dure."

Which means, "There is no bad thing which lasts forever."

And Isa was right—life continued to get better and better from that point on. I started writing again, dated a couple of new guys, and spent time with my friends and family. Slowly but surely, I reengaged with all the parts of my life that I used to love.

With enough time, I became happy.

Happy single.

All on my own.

I never knew, or had forgotten, I should say, that I could make myself happy. It isn't anyone else's job but mine. Whether I meant to or not, I had bought the lie that meeting someone and getting married would make me happy. All the romantic movies, questions about when I was going to meet someone, and the glorification of marriage and family had seeped in, and I believed finding love is the only way to find true happiness.

Once I got rid of the idea that I *needed* marriage in order to be happy, I was freed up to go make the life I wanted.

I learned this lesson in the context of singleness. What's interesting is that at thirty, a few of my friends who got married young are learning this same lesson in the context of marriage. They got the husband, the house, and the kids, and they aren't happy. It's true whether you are single or married—other people and things aren't designed to play this role in our lives. You have to make you happy. And it looks different for everyone.

I've become protective of my happiness. I try not to take for granted some of my favorite things:

Sleeping in on Saturday

Enjoying my leftovers the next day

Watching mass amounts of Hallmark movies with my
    mom at Christmas with no one judging me

Spending my money however I want

Eating an avocado for dinner

Listening to my music

Blasting the heater in the car

Knowing that any clutter in my room is *mine*

Not shaving every day

Taking girls' nights for granted

Getting ready for a date

Booking a flight without consulting anyone else

Ordering onions and/or garlic at dinner guilt-free

Having the option to move to a new city if I want

No man hair in my sink

Dancing with a stranger

Living with my best friends
Flirting
Dishing the good, the bad, the ugly after a date
Sleeping in the middle of the bed with all the covers
Red lipstick without smudges
Not knowing how my story will end

I've noticed something wonderful about the single women in my life. Inside each of them is a courageous desire to experience a full life, beyond marriage. Quite frankly, they want it all. My guess is that if you're reading this book, you know it's in you too. It's the part of you that won't let you settle, the part that is *choosing* to wait and is holding on to your independence.

This doesn't mean you won't one day settle down, or be happy when you do. It certainly doesn't mean everyone who got married young shouldn't have or is now unhappy. All I know is I sincerely hope, as you experience the fun and often messy season of dating, you never doubt or ignore the voice inside that says, "I'm not going to give me up to just anybody."

Chapter 6

Jesus, There Are No Men

*Why are there so many great American women
and no great American men?*

—Carrie,
Sex in the City

Name: Amy
Age: 30
Occupation: Personal trainer
City: Seattle

— — —

Dear friend,

Oh man, what a mess. It all started out so well. Coming from a divorced family, I've always been very independent. I didn't date much through high school and college. Between school, Young Life leading, working, and figuring out what thriving career I wanted to have in which big city, I didn't think too much about which guy might be worth messing up my plans for. Then it happened: I met a guy who caught my attention. Before I knew it, I was in a relationship, a Christian relationship. Unbeknownst to me, this came with an incredible amount of pressure and questions I had no answers for: Is this what I want forever? What is it supposed to feel like when you are with "the one"? Are we doing this right? Amid all these questions, I found it difficult to just be present in the relationship, and it eventually ended when he moved away.

I quickly found myself back at square one, focused on career, on where and who I wanted to be. I was out of school, had my first real job and no homework, and then it finally came: the desire for a companion. For the first time in my life, I wanted someone I could share life with. Rather than just making Amy plans, I wanted to make us plans. I had heard other girls refer to this before, but the idea was totally foreign to me. My Amy plans were always awesome enough on their own.

One day, I met him. Everything was so easy, fun, and better. Long distance made it difficult, but talking to him was so easy, the hours would fly by. Traveling every other weekend was worth it. Talking with friends and mentors about how to move along through the relationship, I heard all the familiar lines: "When you know, you know." "Do you need more time to figure out how you feel about him?"

I thought this must be it; I had never felt this way before. It made sense to start taking things a little more seriously: spending the holidays with his family, talking engagement, and relocating. It's all fun and games until someone gets cold feet. Especially when it's not you.

In six months, I had gone from hopeful to heartbroken. It was over. He had changed his mind, and I couldn't handle his doubt. My fear of being abandoned was suffocating. First my dad, and now him—everybody leaves. I couldn't do it. I could never be that vulnerable or hopeful ever again. It was too risky and too painful. Even the thought of risking this pain again was too much.

I returned to my MO: running, new plans, new city, and new job. In my new space, I started to face my disillusionment and, even worse, myself. Was this dating and relationship thing supposed to be this painful and this difficult?

I still don't have an answer to this. In fact, I feel like I have fewer answers now than I did when I was twenty. Relationships, both dating and friendships, are hard but fun, weird yet interesting, and that is exactly what they are supposed to be. I don't think every dating relationship is supposed to end in marriage, nor do I think you need to be thinking marriage with every relationship. There is value in every date and every relationship regardless of where it ends up. Not everyone is going to love you, and the sooner you can embrace that and be okay with it, the better off you will be in the dating minefield. The opinion of others doesn't make us who we are. As cheesy as it may sound, your relationship with Jesus is the only relationship that can consistently speak to this identity longing. For me, I feel that living rooted in him is the best way to stay levelheaded while navigating things that have no map.

We are in this together!

Amy

P.S. "To bestow on them a crown of beauty instead of ashes, the oil of joy instead of mourning, and a garment of praise instead of a spirit of despair. They will be called oaks of righteousness, a planting of the LORD for the display of his splendor" (Isa. 61:3).

- -

After Europe, I reentered the dating pool. And let me tell you, sometimes the pool is contaminated. Like oil-spill, all-the-ducks-are-dying contaminated.

Finding the right guy feels ~~hard~~ impossible. Many of my friends married their first boyfriends. Me, not so much. I've dated—and redated—my share of no's while attempting to stay open to the possibility that my Mr. Right is out there.

As the months pass, my list grows:

Taylor: consumed too much creatine and Red Bull
Christian: didn't like me back
James #1: our conversation didn't flow well.
James #2: didn't like me back
Brad: hung up on his ex
Kyle #1: not a Christian
Aaron: going another direction in life
Reese: cornered me in a serious conversation while I was
trying to fast dance to a Beyonce song at a wedding
Brett: partied too hard
Kyle #3: Peter Pan syndrome
Travis: wanted to quit his job and "live off the land"

Each time, things didn't work out. Sometimes I knew exactly why, and sometimes I didn't. Sometimes it hurt; sometimes I was relieved. Sometimes they liked me and I didn't feel the same. Sometimes they weren't into me.

And that's life.

With the closing of each relationship, the search for a new one eventually begins. Every time I step out, I remember the phenomenon. You know. The Phenomenon. The universe's sick joke of having more awesome single women than single men. Somehow we all know a ton of great single girls and no nontoxic single guys. How is that possible? Was there some type of reverse China in the eighties that no one talks about?

There are plenty of more plausible theories—delayed adolescence, the economy, our culture is terrible at raising men. Rather than fumble my way through, I asked a few of my guy friends to give input. They by no means can speak for every guy, but they do a better job than I can, being a female and all.

Dear Davey, Jon, and Rob:

Why aren't you married yet? That's all.

Cheers,

Cindy

— — —

Hi, Cindy [Rob is thirty and works in the entertainment industry]:

Considering that getting married is something I think I would do and maybe even want to do, why haven't I done it yet? The simple answer is that I just haven't found what I am looking for.

Though true to my experience, that answer is probably not detailed enough to be informative or useful, so what follows is my attempt at a more in-depth explanation. Hopefully it makes some sense!

One big reason that I haven't gotten married yet is that I want to have a certain kind of connection with a woman if I am going to marry her, and I haven't found that yet. I don't really know how to explain what that means other than to say that I want to want her, and I want her to want to be with me.

That sentiment needs a bit of unpacking if you are to fully understand what I mean by it. By "want to want her," I mean that I want to want her in the fullest sense. Not just sexually, though that is a part of it. I want to want her in the fullness of who she is. I want to never want to stop learning about her. I want to have a connection so deep that I can't deny it. I want to be compelled to put her interests and wants before mine. I want to think about her when I think about the future. I realize that this is probably a high standard, and I'm not sure I'll ever find it. That said, if the kind of thing I've described isn't out there, then what's the point?

When I say that "I want her to want to be with me," I mean that I don't have any clue what goes into this sort of decision for women, or any specific woman, and so it would be unfair for me to say what they need to want out of it other than to want to be with me. If I can get to the place I've described in a relationship with a woman, then I will try everything in my power to make sure they are getting whatever it is that they need out of it.

For me, that is enough. I think I've had parts of what I am describing with different people at different points, but it has never been all the way there. The day I find a woman I want in the way I have described, and who wants to be with me, I will ask her to marry me. I just haven't found her yet.

Best,

Rob

— — —

Well, hello, Cindy [Davey is thirty-two and is a worship pastor]:

I'm that rare, strange guy who has wanted to get married since he was about six years old. Singleness was never an option in my mind. I believed some little girl would love my Ninja Turtles shirt and MC Hammer pants as much as I did, and together we'd ride off into the sunset on a Big Wheel while quoting *Back to the Future*.

In my quest for such things, I've learned a lot about myself and what it means to be a man. More often than not, it came from those times when I've fallen flat on my face and learned exactly what *not* to do. Why am I not married? Well, I'm someone who is waiting, just like you are. Waiting for what, you ask?

True love.

Yeah, I still believe in it.

I probably shouldn't anymore, but I do.

Have you ever listed a used diamond ring on eBay? No one sells a used diamond ring for happy reasons, and neither did I. After proudly hollowing out my bank account to make one girl's dreams come true, I was now selling the remnant of my mistakes and poor choices to whichever cheap, lovestruck opportunist deemed it acceptable to start a marriage using the symbol of another man's broken dreams.

I shouldn't believe in true love. Not after that. But I still do.

It was my choice. The choice to pop the question and also the choice to change my mind. To willfully break all the lofty promises I had made to her was excruciating. Love doesn't just undo itself. It took months and years for each painful layer to unravel. Each new milestone came with its own set of pain and freedom. Her birthday, Thanksgiving, Christmas, the day we had planned to get married—each a new wave of failure.

My pursuit of love failed because I had no idea who I was in the first place.

Who am I? Who are you? What are we doing here?

A man's well-being is intimately attached to his identity. Most every problem a man has can be traced to a point in his life where he lost sight of who he is.

We live in a world of conflicting messages, even within the Christian world. Men, whether it's spoken or unspoken, are told who to be and how to conduct themselves. While it's helpful to hear these things from the pulpit, who are we really listening to? In an ocean of noise, what voice have we zeroed in on?

Traditionally this has been a boy's father, but sadly, some traditions don't always carry on. We all know our culture is lacking in the good-father department. As of the 2010 census, more than one-third (more than fifteen million) of America's children are growing up without a father. Fatherlessness is an epidemic in our culture, and its ripple effect is vast and devastating.

When it comes to relationships and marriage, how can one know what type of person we are looking for if we don't know what type of person we are? How can we know what to strive for when we don't have a model? It's difficult to hit the mark when you yourself are a moving target. And through no fault of your own, a man could be sitting across the table from you and not be into it at all because he hasn't yet answered his own identity question.

In the months following my broken engagement, I felt like an infant. Broken, weak, naked, and poor. All my comforts and consistencies had been stripped away. So often we define ourselves by our relationships, accomplishments, possessions, or surroundings. Through a "coincidental" series of events, I was left without a job, car, home, or fiancee. Half of my friends left me, and the other half were distant from neglect after four years of pouring myself into a girlfriend. I was lost, confused, and alone. Yet those severely wounded months were some of the most precious months of my life. I realized I had to get right myself before I could lead anyone anywhere except toward destruction. My manhood mission had begun, and with dry eyes and stumbling steps, I looked for a picture of what it means to be a man. What I found were many barriers.

You ladies need to know that most of the men around you are unfamiliar with your true worth. They live in a society that preaches how easy it is to attain the things they've always wanted. They are not used to the idea of having to work for them. And let's just put it out there: relationships are hard work. Most men aren't used to such a concept. Most men are used to things coming easily. Our society has done a bang-up job of creating man-boys. Training them that things like morality and work ethic are old-fashioned and outdated. So without working very hard for something, it'll just appear right in front of you and satisfy all your wildest desires.

And the kicker is, because you didn't give any of your time, energy, or money to it, you don't value it. It was too easy.

If you really want the kind of man in your life who is willing to put in the hard, necessary work to make you his, don't be easy.

I'm serious.

Don't allow yourself to be low-hanging fruit. Don't view yourself as easy to attain. The right kind of man will be hopelessly attracted to a woman who treats herself with dignity. The wrong kind of man will lust after the woman with a low view of herself. The wrong kind of man is like a shark that smells blood in the water. He can sense brokenness in his wounded prey. His selfishness knows no bounds. His perceived affection for you isn't about you at all, and once you cease to fulfill his needs, he'll move on to the next one. For the wrong kind of guy, you are a means to an end. To the right kind of guy, you *are* the end.

Be the woman who understands her true worth. I'm begging you. Don't settle. As hard as it may be, never sell yourself short. There are men out there who maybe just need a challenge. Be the kind of woman who, by her own conduct, challenges a man to step up his game. Be the woman who makes him become a better man. The right man should be willing to go to the ends of earth to make you his. If he's not willing to do that, let him walk away. If you lower your standards and make things easier on him, he won't value you as much.

Don't settle.

It's hard out there, for the women and the men. I'll never forget that moment when I finally realized that this world is an ever-shifting landscape and that my identity needs to be rooted in the unchanging, unwavering love of God. Without this anchor, I'll be tossed by any wave that happens to roll by. Until I hold to my identity in Christ, I'll never be at peace, I'll never be content, and I'll never be able to love anyone the way I was designed to.

So yes, I still believe in true love.

I believe it's real, not just a fancy dream. Why? Because I believe God is true love. And he never breaks a promise.

Sincerely,

Davey

— — —

Hey [Jon is thirty-two and a baseball player]:

I definitely thought that by age thirty-two I would be married. I think there were a lot of things that went wrong for me not to be married at my age. I was in love with a girl I probably should have married in my early twenties, but at that time, pursuing a career as a professional baseball player was all I could think about, as far as my future was concerned. I went away to play and was a horrible boyfriend. Of course she threatened to break up with me, and by the time I finally realized she was serious, she had moved on. I still think about her today ten years later.

Being single and twenty-three, I felt like I had all the time in the world to find a wife. For some reason, the single life to me meant being in bars trying to pick up girls. So I spent the next seven years having two- to three-week relationships. I did meet some very nice girls, girls I am a fool not to have taken seriously. At that point in my life, I wasn't their type anyway. They were out at the bar occasionally, and when they figured out I was out every night, spending all my money on beer, it was a big red flag. I feel like girls need a certain level of security, but all they were getting from me at the time was a drunk who lived day-to-day with enough cash to buy them a drink and a cab ride home.

Thankfully, things have changed over the past couple of years. I no longer drink or go to bars. I also don't date anymore, mainly because I am trying to fix the financial ruin that seven years of partying creates. I now have found myself out of debt, sober, employed, and things seem to be looking up. I'm thankful God didn't give up on me.

Now, at thirty-two, it's hard to meet a woman. I no

longer go to bars, online doesn't fit me, and at church it seems like all the girls my age are married. I sometimes wonder if I am not married simply because I missed my window.

Jon

Well, there you have it—men find the dating and marriage world just as confusing and challenging as we do. It's clear we both fare better when we have a sense of who we are before taking on a relationship.

Though the feminist side of us might hate to admit it, in many ways, meeting a husband provides identity and direction for a woman. It answers a lot of questions for us—if we'll have kids, who we will raise them with, where we will live, what our lifestyle will be. It is the opposite for men. For them, taking on a woman introduces a lot of questions: Am I ready to be a dad? What kind of career do I need in order to give her the lifestyle she wants? Can I do it? Do I want this responsibility? They may ask themselves many of these questions while single, but you throw in a woman, and she brings the pressure to have answers.

We women, too, have to know who we are. For us, this looks like having a strong sense of our value. When we do, we can better protect our hearts and emotional stability.

In dating, knowing your value means expecting him to go the distance to be with you. You are worth his giving up some of his wants and desires for yours. The crazy part is that anything short of this isn't going to be satisfying for you *or for him*. A good guy actually wants to find a girl who draws this type of sacrifice out of him.

Which is why the message "he's just not that into you" is in fact very helpful. If he's not making an effort to ask you out or get to know you as more than friends, walk away. If you're in a relationship and he won't take steps forward when the time is right, walk away. If you are chasing him, pursuing him, putting in more time or money than him (this goes for minutes spent obsessing about him), stop. Wait for a guy who is crazy about you! They want to be crazy about you!

Don't be easy.

In the summers during high school, I lifeguarded at a Christian camp. We all lived in the cabins and hung out after our shifts. As you can imagine, camp love ran wild. It was three months of nonstop proximity crushing. (A proximity crush is when you think you like someone because you see him or her all the time in an isolated environment.) For all the fun and butterflies, there was a fair share of heartache and hurting one another.

One night, our dorm mom shared at our girls' Bible study a lesson on dating. "Be the kind of woman a guy wants to be with. Pray and hold out for a spiritual leader." (Still don't know what the heck that means.) And last but not least, "Don't dress in a way that makes him stumble. The right guy will be looking for a good girl who loves the Lord."

We all left that night with great reminders on how to be a good Christian girl. From what I was told, the guys spent their night discussing avoiding porn and masturbation. All of us met up in the malt shop later with absolutely no new information on how to treat each other.

Christian dating advice tends to be very me-centered. The idea is that if you make yourself the right person, God will bring the right mate into your life. While that may be true, it doesn't give any handholds for surviving the in-between.

When I was younger, I thought Christian guys who professed to love God were good guys. Which meant they would make good boyfriends. Turns out they can still be afraid of commitment, always want the next best thing, and see me as an object no matter what I wear. It would've been helpful to know that good guys do not always know how to have good relationships. No amount of prayer, Bible study, or one-piece bathing suits was going to change that. I had to be the one to set boundaries. And not just purity boundaries—those we all heard a lot of. What I needed was a lesson on commitment boundaries—when and where to give my heart and time.

These days, I try very hard not to put up with more crap than I should. No more shady cancelling of plans, wishy-washy feelings toward me, or confusion about what we are doing together and where we are going.

I also give all guys the motorcycle test. The motorcycle test is a gem I came up with while dating a guy named Brett, which I'll get to in a moment.

First, if you've never read the book *Love and Respect* by Emerson Eggerichs, I recommend it. The major premise is that women need love and men need respect. A lot of times women give love when what actually makes a man feel good is respect. Many men, on the other hand, have an easier time giving women respect than giving love.

I read the book while dating Jake and had a hard time picturing what it looked like to respect a man. I knew ways to show Jake love, but not respect. Respect was a nice word in theory, but how did it play out in the day-to-day? What did respecting the guy I was dating feel like?

Answers to these questions didn't come until I met Brett. He was very successful and extremely happy. His excitement for life was infectious. On our second date, he said he was thinking about buying a motorcycle, and I listened calmly as he chatted about the details.

I later found my reaction, or I should say nonreaction, intriguing. *Huh, I have absolutely no problem with this guy buying a motorcycle.* Now had Jake said he wanted one, tons of internal alarms would have sounded. Questions about all the things he needed to think through and probably hadn't thought of yet would have spilled out: "Can you afford it? Do you know you need a special license? Do you have time to go get that license? Have you ever even driven a motorcycle? Who is going to help you choose one?" And on and on it could endlessly go.

Without even giving it a thought, I knew Brett well enough to know he had gone over all the details. He knew how to make wise decisions, handle his finances, and go for things he wanted in life. In short, I respected him.

As time went on, I realized that for me, respect looks like trusting a man to handle himself and others. It's believing he can not only make smart decisions but also make them from a healthy place. The men I respect don't do things for attention or to please others. They can separate from the crowd and resist the pressure of friends. They know how to make plans and follow through on them. They know how to fail, pick up the pieces, and start again.

Of course, no one is perfect, but I believe we can have

a sense about a man, and it's important to be with someone you respect, especially if you are considering building a life with him. You want to trust that he'll do what is best for you and your relationship on his own.

Men need to be respected. A second-guessing and untrusting girlfriend cuts a man down and picks away at his confidence. That was one of my biggest mistakes with Jake. I shouldn't have dated him, because I didn't respect him. I wanted to be in a relationship, and so instead of walking away, I stayed and subjected him to all kinds of disrespect. I was constantly hoping he'd "learn this," "figure out that," and "pull his crap together," and it wasn't fair to him. Had he behaved that way toward me, I would have felt awful about myself, and I don't ever want to be that type of girlfriend again.

So every guy I date gets the motorcycle test.

I'm not kidding. At some point, I look at him and think, "Okay, Cindy, pretend he has just turned to you and said, 'I'm thinking of getting a motorcycle.'"

And then I listen for the alarms.

If they ring, I walk away. It's not always easy, but I'm learning to obey my gut when it's telling me someone isn't the right fit for me. No more guys I want to teach or change, no more inappropriate friendships, and no more men who are indecisive about me. I've set the bar high so that only the ones who truly want to jump can reach it.

#Ishouldveknownwhen

Disclaimer: #Ishouldveknownwhen is a list my friends and I have put together to describe the exact moment we knew it just wasn't going to work out with a guy. These are true events from actual dates. Enjoy!

1. He showed up to our date on rollerblades.
2. He still shared a bedroom with his sister.
3. I found out he was born in the nineties.
4. Sent me a shirtless selfie.
5. Takes shirtless selflies.
6. He told his friends we were together after our third date.
7. LOVED vikings.
8. He asked me to drive myself to our first date. An hour away. Where he lived.
9. Wore more jewelry than me.
10. He wouldn't sign up for a trial gym membership because three months was "too much commitment."
11. I googled his name and discovered he was famous in the gay blogging community as an underwear model.
12. He introduced me to his cats. Plural.
13. At dinner he referred to me as his "sister in Christ."
14. Had a girl best friend.
15. Toward the end of our first date, he invited me to Thanksgiving.
16. He told me his New Year's resolution was to do more yoga. When I asked why, he replied, "To be honest, it's to pick up girls." #classy

17. I found his blog where he wrote about proposing to his friend even though they never had dated. #shesaidno #sodidi

18. He told me about his addiction to dip. (I thought he was talking about chips.)

19. He fought in the Gulf War. (How old do you think I am?)

20. I asked him what he did for fun in college, and he said, "I don't know. I ate a lot."

21. I asked where he was from, and he replied, "The Kingdom of Tonga."

22. He said he needed to know within two days of meeting a girl if he could marry her. #slowitdownbuddy

23. He kept his last girlfriend a secret.

24. He angrily chucked his pizza into the middle of the street because I wouldn't sit on his lap. (It was our second date.)

25. He took me to a food bank for our third date.

26. He texted me three Bible verses and two devos after our first date.

27. He told me he was an actor. (He was a waiter.)

28. He used the word courting.

29. I saw his tribal tattoo.

30. He claimed to never eat vegetables and was annoyed I didn't order a soda.

31. He called me dude.

32. I thought he had special needs but later found out it was just an accent.

33. Only listened to Christian music.

34. He had more hair products than me.

35. I knew more about camping than he did.
36. He was a self proclaimed "cocktail guy."
37. He got political on Facebook.
38. He used more emojis than me.
39. His jeans had jewels on the pockets.
40. He wouldn't take his Bluetooth off in the restaurant.
41. He said he did "freelance stuff" for a job. AKA unemployed.
42. He called to see what county I lived in before coming to pick me up. When I asked him why, he replied, "I don't want my ankle bracelet to go off."
43. Karate was the main topic of conversation.
44. The *L* word was dropped wayyyyy to early.
45. He consistently referred to himself in the third person.
46. Swore all the time on social media.
47. He had a thumb ring on. Ew.
48. He joined a social group online called Vegas Pool Party Lovers.

Chapter 7

Grown-Up Sex Talk

Love is the answer, but while you are waiting for the answer,
sex raises some pretty good questions.

—Woody Allen,
New York Times, Dec. 1975

Name: Keturah
Age: 31
Occupation: Hairstylist
City: Costa Mesa, California

— — —

Dear sister,

If you're anything like me, I never thought I'd be single at thirty-one. Twenty-four—maybe. Twenty-six—definitely a possibility. But by thirty—surely I'd meet someone by thirty, right? Well, not quite. I've met several someones over the years but have never dated anyone for longer than three months, and even that was the exception to the usual one to three dates. When I was growing up in the church, marriage always seemed to be elevated, and singleness was just a club everyone was hoping to get out of, praying they didn't have the "gift of singleness." I always hated that phrase and have many times found myself praying it wasn't a gift I was given.

However, as I was approaching my thirties, I found myself

reflecting on what a gift the season of singleness had been during my twenties. I stopped thinking about it as a lifelong gift and saw it as something I needed right then.

Just because I am a strong, successful woman doesn't mean that I have this magical gift of not wanting to have a family or someone to share my life with. It doesn't mean I'm not attracted to men, and it definitely doesn't mean I don't want to have sex.

I started having sex when I was twenty-five. It wasn't a heat of the moment decision but something that had been building over years of toying with "the line" and believing lies about what would make me attractive and desirable. I often wish I could have coffee with twenty-four-year-old Keturah and convey just a fraction of the pain those early choices led to. It wasn't just about having sex, because the behavior itself was only just covering up the pain and broken-ness I was feeling inside. I'd cycle through regret, shame, and grace, and it was years before I took the hard steps toward true healing. Being sexually active has left me struggling not to feel like anything more than "damaged goods," and even now I have to regularly remind myself not to settle for less than God's best for me, which I often still fail at. I've experienced a lot of pain from my choices through the years, but this deep pain continues to lead me to even deeper healing, and I have more confidence now in my identity as a daughter of God because of it. I have more to give my community and someday my family because of this gift of not being married yet. Hours of journaling, mornings alone with Jesus, and weekends away have saved my life. I could not have found this kind of depth with Jesus without this time. And he's obviously still not done with me.

At the end of the day, the Lord's timing has never been off. When it all comes together, it's clear why I needed to wait. Most days I feel okay with the wait, but I still struggle, wondering whether I will ever meet anyone. I very much want a partner, and I deeply desire to have kids, but for now I'm learning to hold these hopes loosely and am trying to wait well each day.

Ultimately, what I come back to is my trust in Jesus. Not trusting him for a family or a successful career but simply trusting that as I walk with him, he will make things good. I learned long ago that my good and his good aren't always in line — and his good is always better. I am so grateful that the Lord didn't answer my prayers about guys I've wanted to marry over the years. Anthony and I would have been married way too young. Steve and I would have been a disaster together. Tim didn't age so well and decided to move to Vegas. Jeff is way too dramatic for me, and Jesse never would have let me buy a Range Rover.

This season of my life is a gift. One of my closest friends just recently got married at thirty-seven. I learned a lot from watching her wait well. She often reflected on the parallel to waiting well for Christ to return. The journey with Christ throughout Scripture is always marked by waiting and hoping. To be present in my singleness, not wishing away this season, is glorifying to God and reminds me of what I'm ultimately waiting for.

We will always be waiting for something until Christ

returns. If you find yourself in a similar place, wait well with me in this season. The Lord is good and hasn't forgotten about you. Enjoy the things you're able to do right now, embrace this season, don't be afraid to speak out your desires, and hold loosely the things you wish for. He sees you, he knows you, and he's working it all out for your good and the good of those around you.

Much love,

Keturah

Name: Katie
Age: 30
Occupation: High school teacher
Location: Los Angeles

— — —

Hello,

I'm thirty and I've never been kissed. This isn't typically the kind of information I share when introducing myself, but I think it's important you know. I never set out to be a thirty-year-old kissing virgin. It just kind of happened. In high school, there weren't any boys worth kissing, and I was content spending Friday nights with my girlfriends lip-syncing to the Backstreet Boys. In college, I met plenty of other fun and normal girls who were kissing virgins, so I didn't panic as my roommates found guys to date and I found myself as a constant third, fifth, and even seventh wheel. Then after college, when all my friends were saying "I do," I still didn't worry because I was certain that my guy was just around the corner. But he wasn't.

I tried eHarmony, I tried dating my best friend, and I've been set up on some ridiculously awful and some seemingly wonderful blind dates. But still, nothing. Nada. Oh, and there was that one time I accidentally ended up on a date with a forty-seven-year-old janitor from Compton, but that's another story. When I was in my midtwenties, I was sad and confused and, quite frankly, a little pissed about my singleness. It didn't seem right or fair that everyone else had found their husbands and I couldn't even find a boyfriend. I got sucked into comparing my journey with others' and ended up throwing a lot of bitter pity parties.

It took me years to learn the simple lesson that God is greater than I ever imagined and that I am not nearly as important as I thought. Don't get me wrong; I know that I am a chosen, beloved daughter of the King. But I was twenty-seven before I realized that I am not a princess in some fairytale love story. It took me way too long to discover that God's plans for me are much bigger than simply finding a husband. He wants to transform me and shape me into one who can be used for his kingdom and his glory, and this does not require a man and a wedding band.

I'm sure you've heard the well-intentioned encouragement that "his plans are better" and "his timing is perfect." And if you're like me, you probably know it's true but still kind of hate hearing it. I mean, I'm thirty and my baby-making years are slipping away. How can that be good timing, God? But then I sit in his presence and remember that he is King and I am not. And his kingdom is about him, not me. So as his daughter and his servant, I can live my single life with joy because I'm living it with purpose and with him. I can live a joyful life *today* because of the future God has promised me — not necessarily the one I want with a prince and a castle and some quirky little blond kids but the one that he wants for me. And the more I understand his heart, the more I want that future for me too.

I know how hard this single life can be, and I know you may get angry with God and men and the whole single life. I know you may get sucked into comparing your life with others' and throwing the single-girl pity party, but when you do, I hope you remember that we trust a good God who has good plans, even if those plans are very different from our own. Even if those plans involve being a thirty-year-old kissing virgin. Because what I've discovered, and hope you do too, is that we don't have to wait for a husband to arrive in order to find happiness. No sir, our happily-ever-after doesn't depend on a prince; it arrived the day we said yes to our King. Now if we can just remember that and live like it's true! That's my prayer for me and for you.

Sincerely,

Your sister Katie (aka the thirty-year-old kissing virgin)

— —

In my closet there are lots of items. On the far left, all my jackets and sweaters hang side by side. To the right are all my blouses, arranged by color, followed by my dresses. The drawers below are pretty standard: pants, workout attire, socks and underwear.

At a glance, it all looks very normal and neat. What you wouldn't know, unless you are me, is that toward the back are all my "going out options," as I call them. Separate from my church clothes and work go-tos, these outfits are tighter, cut lower, and sexier. I wear them only on a night out. I would never wear them on a Sunday morning. Similarly, I would feel like a troll in my church clothes at a bar. One section never sees daylight; the other never goes out after dark.

It's just clothes, and it's just a closet. But for me, it represents where I've subconsciously put all of my sex life.

Separate.

Toward the back.

Private.

I'm not exactly sure why I separate it. No one told me to. It just seems to be the way my circle of friends lives. We all have a sex life, whether we are having intercourse or not. I don't consider a person's sex life to be just sex. I consider it to be everything from attraction to intimacy to body image. All of it plays a part. And most of us don't talk about it—not really. Most of my friends and I seem to understand sexuality is complicated, and we prefer to let each other make our own choices privately. But at what cost?

David Kinnaman explores this phenomenon in his book *You Lost Me*. One girl says, "I feel like my church and youth group compartmentalized everything, and so I did too. Here's your faith in this pigeonhole. Here's your education. Here's your work cubicle, and there's your family. Over there is sex, all by itself behind a curtain. I feel like becoming an adult is this painful process of decategorizing my life. There are no categories. There is just life."[3]

I tend to like categories because they feel safe and more manageable. If my spiritual life seems in good shape — going to church, tithing, reading my Bible, etc. — but I'm feeling guilt over my sex life, I can separate them and still feel okay about the rest. It works in reverse too. If my spiritual life is out of whack — I'm prideful, selfish, prone to anger, etc. — but am pure in my sex life, I can separate it and feel good about being pure. Once we admit that everything is connected, we have to look at everything as a whole. Sex becomes tied to and evenly weighted with kindness, honesty, and faithfulness. "Bad Christians have sex and good Christians do not" no longer applies. We are left with Christians who do good and bad things for all kinds of reasons.

If I talk about sexuality in a sex box, I can give simple biblical answers to others and walk away feeling good. Don't have sex before you are married. And as long as everyone gets married before their frontal lobe fully develops, we have decent odds of making it to the altar unscathed. But what if you don't get married at twenty? What if you spend five, ten, fifteen-plus years as a single adult? When you're older and single, you're forced to wrestle with a more complex scenario. Sexuality is more complicated and vulnerable when you find yourself in several different relationships throughout your singleness. It becomes increasingly harder to buy (and live with) a Sunday school answer to a Friday night question.

It is hard enough to answer sexuality questions for yourself. Dating adds the additional struggle of mixing your thoughts with someone else's. I'm not sure how it was when my parents dated; perhaps thirty years ago, Christians all agreed to wait till marriage. What I do know is that nowadays, dating a Christian guy does not mean we think the same about sex. According to a study conducted by Christian Mingle and JDate, 61 percent of self-identifing Christians said they would have sex before marriage; 56 percent said it is okay to move in together after dating for awhile.[4] One study I read said 80 percent of single Christians between the ages of eighteen and twenty-nine have had sex, which is nearly the same rate as the 88 percent of non-Christians who have had sex outside of marriage.[5] All that is to say that even if you're dating within the church, you still have to talk about your expectations.

We ask questions like, "He's had six partners; is that a lot?" and, "Should I kiss him if he's not my boyfriend?" and, "Can we sleep in the same bed and not have sex, or is that wrong?" and, "We love each other; is sex *that* big of a deal?"

In my experience, the church breezes by the conversation, perhaps hoping to give the purity youth group talk to a bunch of thirty-year-olds, most of whom have already had sex. Which is why you and I are all over the map. It's why sexuality, and all its clothing, is shoved in the back of the closet.

If the studies are correct, four out of five of you reading this have had sex, and the rest of you are waiting. Everyone holding this book is at a different spot in what you believe and how you act when it comes to sex. Regardless of where that is, I still believe God wants the best for us all. The things he tells us to do, not to do, to watch out for, or to be intentional about are for our good. He's clear about the best way to handle sex—have it with the one guy who has made a commitment to be your husband and provider for the rest of your life. That is the environment where you and I will feel the safest amd most loved and treasured. I imagine that even in a marital covenant there is plenty of awkwardness, insecurities, and differing expectations. That's why the highest form of commitment makes this best-case scenario.

Maybe you believed in waiting once a long time ago, or maybe you never even considered it. Maybe you agree but choose to have sex anyway. Maybe you've never been kissed. It's just all so complicated.

I struggled over how to approach this chapter for months. For those of you who are waiting, I don't want you to feel like you are weird, out of date, or alone. For those of you who have had sex, I don't want you to read this and feel judged or unwelcome. I believe we could all, regardless of our past, sit around a table and agree that sex and sexuality are at work in our relationships. What unites all of us, no matter where we are on the spectrum of beliefs and behavior, is that every one of us is sexual, even if we aren't having sex. Sexuality is part of being human. For a woman, wanting to be sexy or desirable goes hand in hand with wanting to be beautiful. It's a healthy part of growing up.

When you are single, what do you do with that part of yourself? The part that is made to feel sexy while single. Suppress it and hope we get married soon? Just do whatever feels best in the meantime? Somewhere between these extremes, there's a way to live. To have our sex lives, and our closets, be a bit more fluid and a little less compartmentalized. I believe it starts with honest conversations. Not with the whole world or even on social media. But with the people in our lives who know us best. The ones we trust and who can tell us the truth about intimacy, sexuality, and how to be good to ourselves and the people we date.

For the Girls with Underwear That Never Sees the Light of Day

I wrestled with whether to get into my sexual history, because aside from not wanting to alienate anyone, I think it's private and personal. Our media has made sexual history cheaply public. Even those who come out as waiting have been made, or want to be made, into spectacles. In the end, who you sleep or don't sleep with with isn't everyone's business. Bottom line.

As I attempted to write this chapter several times *without* my story, it became flat and surfacey. The very things I didn't want it to be. I kept thinking, Can I really complain about avoiding the subject of sex and then dodge it in my own work? So here we go.

My first two boyfriends wanted to wait before I met them. They had slept with girlfriends in the past but had since felt that God wanted them to do things differently in their next relationships. With the same goal in mind, we did not sleep together.

My next boyfriend was a different story. He and I had one of my best first dates ever. He was happy, confident, and we were going the same direction in life. (Bonus points—a firefighter.) We went out a couple of times and made out after our third date. At that point, I could tell the firefighter wasn't a virgin. I was certain he'd dump me when he found out I was.

I complained to my roommate Melody the next day. "This just sucks. I'm so over it. I finally meet a great guy and I'm going to lose him over this one stupid thing."

Melody was empathetic but said, "Cindy, if you believe waiting is God's best for you, then it's God's best for the firefighter."

Her words gave me a lot to think about. Did I still believe it was God's best? I wanted to, but I had to admit I wasn't so sure anymore. I had waited so long to meet someone like him. I didn't want to run him off with sex.

During our fourth date, as we sat at the bar, I knew the talk needed to happen. I went with this: "So I know you are a Christian, but everyone feels differently about sex. What do you think about it?"

The firefighter replied, "Well, I've had sex, but I'm not dating you for sex. If you wanted to wait, I'd be willing to do that."

Hold the phone.

I fully realize this makes him an exceptional guy and that not all of them are going to respond this way. But that's how it happened.

I blurted, "Oh, good! Because I'm a virgin!" and immediately cupped my hand over my mouth.

Shocked, he said, "Really? Wow. That's great."

We talked over reasons to wait—it's what we were taught in church, the Bible says to wait, I'm this far along. In the end, we left that night agreeing to date but not sleep together.

As I lay in bed that night, I thanked God for the firefighter's response. I confessed that I hadn't really trusted him (God) and was still conflicted about my own waiting. Melody's words ran through my head as I fell asleep: "If it's God's best for you, then it's God's best for the firefighter." I believed her on one level, but honestly, by that point I was basically holding out only because I had waited this long. It wasn't a spiritual decision for me at that time.

As the firefighter and I we continued to date, I discovered that God had much bigger plans for our decision than I'd expected. The firefighter turned to me several times over the next couple of months and said things like, "I'm glad we are waiting; it takes the pressure off." The guys at his station couldn't believe we weren't sleeping together. and it brought up good conversations. Eventually, the goal to wait became the firefighter's goal too. It wasn't just about me; it was one he said he'd hold to even if he and I didn't work out.

As happy as I was to watch the transformation in my boyfriend, I never anticipated a change in me. I was waiting completely out of obligation. I wasn't happy about it. But God took my bare-minimum obedience and turned it into so much more. Because I had been pretty skeptical of commitment and guys' making empty promises, the fact that the firefighter was willing to wait *for me*, not for his own reasons, helped me trust him. Also, I knew I wanted to date a man of God, but that's super hard to identify. I'd dated enough church guys to know that Christian talk is cheap. Watching God move in the firefighter's life and seeing his evolving desire to be faithful gave me a window into where he stood. I never expected that choosing to wait would've strengthened my relationship both with my boyfriend and with God.

For the Girls with a Lingerie Drawer

I read somewhere that it is easy to judge another person's sin when all your needs are met. I find this so true, especially when we are talking about sex. Married people, depending on the state of their marriage, have the intimacy and emotional and physical validation of a partner. It's easier to say what is right and wrong when you have all those things. It's harder when you don't.

When talking about sex, I've noticed a tendency in the church to talk about it in black and white—you did have sex or you didn't. And while there may be a technical line to cross, it's far more complicated than that. People are motivated to have sex by all kinds of reasons. Maybe things were bad at home and you were looking for somewhere to belong. Maybe you and the guy were truly in love. Maybe you drank too much and went too far. The whys get lost when we talk only in hard lines. But the whys matter to us, and they matter to God.

When we talk about sexual purity without hearing a person's story, it takes a very emotional and physical experience and reduces it to a simple mistake they made or sin they committed. It communicates that this one act makes them a bad Christian. It turns people away from Jesus. It turns people away from forgiving themselves. It turns people away from the idea of waiting.

God knows if you've had sex, but far more important than

that, he knows why you had sex. And I believe God is far more concerned with carefully and delicately handling the whys and where to go from here than getting into the whats (what you have or haven't done and with whom). Maybe you were one of the thousands who made a virginity declaration at a summer camp in seventh grade, only to hide your purity ring at the bottom of a drawer somewhere during freshman year of college. Maybe you're like my roommate, whose parents were appalled she wanted to wait and encouraged her to experience multiple partners. Regardless, I believe God ultimately doesn't see your past when he looks at you. It's not our sexual history he notices first. What he sees are his daughters, and there is so much more to us than who we have been with.

The way we see Jesus treat people in the Bible is meant to show us how Jesus treats us today. One of my favorite stories is from John 4, when Jesus meets a Samairtan woman at a well. In that culture, Jesus wouldn't have been allowed to talk to her because (A) she was a woman and (B) she wasn't Jewish. Ignoring all that, Jesus asked her for a drink of water. He wanted to talk with her and build a relationship. They talk for a bit, and he eventually tells her that he knows she has had five husbands and is currently sleeping with a man she isn't married to. What I love about this story is that Jesus knew her situation all along. It never stopped him from breaking the law to spend time with her. Her past was not Jesus' priority. He cared most about offering her a better future.

I asked a close friend of mine to share her own story of navigating sex in a Chrsitian community:

Before becoming a Christian—well, really just before I surrendered my "lifestyle" to Christ (I believed in Jesus but hadn't really decided that I wanted Jesus to be in charge yet)—I had sex with one guy, my high school sweetheart, whom I had dated for four years.

Initially, I wanted to wait for marriage. I have no memory of anyone specifically telling me that was what I should do. I think it was a standard I felt and had overheard was "right."

In high school, I was partying pretty hard, smoking pot and drinking every weekend, yet I was holding on to being a virgin. When I started to think more about it, it didn't make sense to me. I wondered, What's so special about sex? Why am I okay with drinking and smoking pot, but I'm not okay with having sex?

Now, looking back, that's a lot for a seventeen-year-old girl to process. I remember thinking I was so mature and believed I could make right decisions. In reality, I wasn't equipped to navigate all this. I didn't fully understand the consequences. So I decided to have sex. It wasn't a flippant thought that propelled me to run out and have sex with the first guy I saw. I had been dating someone for a long time and thought, I love this guy. We've been together since eighth grade. It's time we had sex.

Honestly, a part of me was just curious what it would be like. Another part of me craved intimacy. Not that my teenage self used that word, but things were happening at home that made me feel alone, and I wanted so badly to be known. I thought having sex might fill that. That's when I lost my virginity—one extremely hot Southern summer night at my boyfriend's lakehouse during a party. And there it went—my innocent, precious, and pure virginity. I didn't feel shame or guilt then, but I knew I had given something away. I couldn't put my finger on it, but I did feel the weight of it that night. I felt both good and bad. I was confused, but also felt relief.

He was the last person I ever had sober sex with. The string of guys that came at the end of my senior year and all of my freshmen year of college are a blurry distant memory that still haunts me today. See, timing sucks sometimes. My best friend from high school died in a car accident two weeks before I left for college, and I lost it. I ran away from God and ran toward anything that would make me feel numb. I couldn't handle the pain.

Truthfully, I don't like thinking about this year. I had sex with a lot of guys, or really a lot of guys had sex with me, because I don't remember many of them. I struggle with what that even means. Is it sex if you were so drunk you didn't participate? Is it rape if you don't remember any of it? Is it really my fault? Sadly, that first year of college ruined sex for me. It lost its value. It lost its preciousness and its sacredness. Not one time was it fun or did it feel good. I couldn't imagine why people wanted to do it so much or why it was even a gift from God. To me, it felt dirty and manipulative. It became something guys wanted that I did, so for a moment, I felt worthy or wanted.

After that year, I hit rock bottom and turned my life to Jesus. With that, I felt compelled to make some changes in my life. Of course, in my mind I knew that Christians don't have sex, so I told myself that I wouldn't do that again until I was married. "Christians don't have sex" box—check. In my mind, sex became this thing I knew I shouldn't do, or wasn't "allowed" to do, if I was going to frequent Christian circles—or be a Christian at all, for that matter. Because, again, Christians don't do *that*. I was now a new creation, so I shouldn't do it or have the desire to.

That mindset worked for me until I met a guy I fell in love with. He was a Christian and he was hot, like really hot, and he chose me. I couldn't understand how I had been so lucky to find such a great guy who also loved Jesus. Jackpot! I knew we weren't ever going to struggle with sex because, hello, he was a Christian and I was a Christian, so of course we weren't going to have sex. But, being the rebellious Christians that we were, we pushed right up to the line, doing anything and everything as long as we didn't actually "do it." That's what you do when you're a horny Christian. You do what you can without having to feel bad about actually "doing it."

But we all know how that story goes, especially if one of the two people involved has had sex before. It's like taking a girl to a bakery while she's on the Atkins diet and telling her to put a donut right on her lips without taking a bite. It's what I call "setting yourself up for failure."

After awhile, I could tell we both wanted to have sex, and I think we were just waiting to see who would cave first. Well, I caved, and he didn't object. And then we began this tumultuous cycle of "slipping" and having sex and then beating ourselves up when we finished. Like I would guilt and shame myself until I was convinced that I was the most horrible person on earth. "How can I keep doing this when I love Jesus so much?" And then enough time would pass, and we would fall back into a false sense of security.

All this time, I was too embarrassed and ashamed to talk about it with my friends. Because Christians don't have sex. And I didn't want to disappoint anyone. So I would just secretly confess to God and try to will myself to be good once again.

Long story short, I fell hard for this guy. And after a while, you guessed it, he broke my heart. And because I had given him that intimate and special part of myself, my heart broke into a million pieces. It had been so long since I trusted someone with that part of me. I thought the next time I willingly had sex with someone, it was all going to be okay. I was wrong. I was wrong to think I was immune to the hurt that comes from having sex with someone without a lasting commitment (marriage). It was a heartbreak I felt deep in my soul. Honestly, I still feel it sometimes, and it's been years.

We played this back and forth game for a long time, and it only got me stuck in a place of feeling pain and unworthiness. Definitely not what God wanted for me. It was a good lesson though. Don't get me wrong—I wish I had waited for my husband. Ugh. Even writing that breaks my heart. Makes me want to crawl into a hole and never date or get married. I feel that way because now as an adult can I see the consequences of my actions. In the past, I had this excuse—I wasn't living as a Christian, I was in pain and drunk. This time, it was with another Christian, and it was for love. And it wasn't worth it; it just wasn't.

But it happened, it's part of my story, and I'm trusting that God is good and he is FOR ME. I know he can redeem this; he already has begun to.

So now I'm this really mature Christian who does everything right in the dating and sex department. Ha. Who am I kidding? It's still a point of struggle for me. But I have learned a lot, and I'm still trying to wrap my head around all the things I've heard from wise people about sex. I thought I could avoid the pain by compartmentalizing it; however, now I've realized how damaging that is. You can't run away from pain forever. I've felt deeply the pain that I believe God was trying to spare me from.

So now what? Well, I am still single and not with that guy anymore. I actually moved to a new city and got excited about the chance of starting over and meeting someone new. I ended up going on a few dates with these two guys. One of the guys ended up not really being on the same page as me when it came to Jesus. The other one was a hundred percent on the same page as me with Jesus. The thing that blew my mind was that Guy 1 really respected my boundaries and never pushed me to do anything sexually. Guy 2 pushed the boundaries, even after I told him twice I was uncomfortable. *What?!*

My advice, ladies, is to figure out beforehand what you think about sex. Don't think about how close to the line can you get; try thinking how far away from the line can you get. It's not black and white. It's not easy, even when you are dating Christian guys. But it *is* so important. You have to fight to trust that God is good and for you, even in this area.

For All of Us, with Our Comfy Clothes Drawer

Dating is hard enough, with or without sex. Whether we have waited or not waited, what's most important is where we put our trust. Do we believe God cares for us more than any man ever will? Are we willing to trust him, even when it's hard? I believe he can redeem any situation and will use anything he can to draw us closer to him. He's good and he wants what's best for us. Whether you date one guy or a hundred, God's love for you will never fail or change. Focus on that and make your decisions from that place.

Chapter 8

What If It Never Happens?

That is part of the beauty of literature. You discover that your longings are universal longings, that you're not lonely and isolated from anyone. You belong.

—F. Scott Fitzgerald

Name: Christine
Age: 30
Occupation: Office manager
City: Oceanside, California

— — —

Hey there, champ:

Let me tell you a few mantras that have stuck in my head as I've thought about and suffered from love:

Put your head down and plow. I believe that this advice is from someone I went to church with who was referring to the story of Ruth, whom Boaz showed favor to when he saw her working diligently for what she valued. (In her case, she was doing physical labor to feed her family.) What I have taken this to mean is that if you're doing what you love, and you're focusing your energy toward what's most important, the right people will notice. This has proven very true for me. By pouring my heart into what I care about, I've gathered some awesome friends, traveled a quirky but ideal-for-me career path, and even met some cool gentlemen.

(I will say, though, that I always think it's funny when we tell women to behave like Ruth when it comes to men. While it worked out for her, please, don't lay down anywhere near where a guy you're trying to woo has passed out drunk.)

Love is a battlefield. This one comes, of course, from Pat Benatar, and it's the truth. A huge reason I haven't invested more time toward finding a relationship is that love is really, really hard. You don't have to be in a romantic relationship to know this; just walk through tough situations with a good friend or family member. While love is incredible and wonderful, it requires you to give up yourself, your selfish motives, and, contrary to all your instincts, prioritize someone else. And to keep doing that every day, forever.

The pickin's are slim out there. I say this to encourage you, because it's true; you probably have experienced this, and if not, you will. A 2010 Barna study confirmed what we already suspected: that for every twenty- to twenty-nine-year-old man who considers faith his top priority, there are six women who feel the same. The numbers are in our favor if we're looking for girls to join a Bible study, but not if we want to get married.

My story:

I haven't had a boyfriend for a looong time. I sometimes think I forgot how to kiss. I had a few boyfriends in high school and college, then spent about two years off and on with the one I thought I'd marry.

Having been dedicated to my faith and my Christian community, I'd been really tame as far as partying and physical intimacy are concerned. I'm happy to say I've never had sex, done drugs, or woken up without remembering the night before. I did have what I consider to be a wild year or so when I was twenty-five-ish. Craving love and attention, I'd go out to bars most weekends, make out with random guys, and date a lot of people who were just wrong for me. (A therapist said I was intentionally choosing men I'd have no future with.) There was this crazy rush as I realized some guy totally thought I was hot and couldn't take his eyes off me.

I was working through a lot of personal stuff at the time, ironically, transitioning into a job in women's ministry and thinking a lot about how God created us uniquely as women. It's amazing, really, how as females we possess the ability to bring comfort, how our beauty and femininity truly have an intoxicating power—and God did that on purpose. Just as every good gift can be misused, I was going through a period of wielding my beauty, femininity, and sexuality as tools, weapons even, to get the attention and affirmation I desired. I know I've basically just described a typical Saturday night across America for lots of people our age, but it's really twisted how so many of us resort to manipulation, when our sexuality and beauty were instead created to bless.

Thankfully, that phase ran its course. After a few quiet years, I briefly dated a super crazy guy who, while devoted to Jesus, was otherwise completely wrong for me. The moral of that story is red flags are red for a reason—pay attention to them. Since then, I've been pretty gun shy when it comes to love but have also gotten much more involved in my own pursuits. I spend a lot of time with this ridiculous and wonderful group of family and friends who surround me, getting to play auntie to lots of sweet babies. I volunteer with the local women's center for victims of abuse. I sew and paint and read and write and post pictures of my dog on the internet, and am super, super content. The idea of dating makes me laugh, and I'm so grateful for this season, because while I'd love to be with someone awesome one day (maybe when I'm forty?), I realize that fitting someone into that huge role will mean taking something else out, and I'd hate to do that.

I have a lot of hope for my future. For one thing, when I look at my mom and her sisters, I realize I'm only going to get better looking. Also, I like myself much more than I did two, five, and ten years ago, and I think that makes me better suited to love someone else, and to evaluate who's worthy of me. I know that if and when someone cool does happen to cross my path, I'll be able to choose to start a relationship not because I feel pressure to or because everyone else is but because I want to, with this person, at this time. That sounds just about right.

All of my love and hope to you, darling, you fighter. You are walking steps that have been worn by good women, and you're leaving a path for many to come behind you. I'm excited to read *your* letter in volume 2.

Christine

- -

Jesus went to a wedding, single, at the age of thirty, and made more wine. This makes so much sense to me. He'd probably been stuck sitting at the oddball table, between his prepubescent cousins and married couples. As if that weren't bad enough, his mom swung by his seat to ask him to help out with the wine. (This could be my diary!) Guests probably speculated about why Jesus still wasn't married after he left. "He's such a great guy. What's the deal?" they all wondered. On this less than ideal evening, Jesus chose to perform his very first recorded miracle. Here, at a wedding. One he attended without a date.

If you've read the story, you know that Jesus turns a bunch of water into top-notch wine. What's interesting about this miracle, when you think about it, is that it isn't about healing a disease, feeding the hungry, or raising someone from the dead. This miracle, his big debut, was about a social grace. It was about saving a father from embarrassment and shame. It was about keeping a bride and groom blissfully unaware that their family had been cheap. It was partially about Jesus getting his mom off his back. Sure, there is more going on here symbolically, but for all the recipients of the miracle that day, it was about avoiding awkwardness and keeping the party going.

There are days when I feel guilty for complaining about my awkward situations. I have so much to be thankful for. When people are suffering from disease, starvation, or abuse, it would seem insignificant, almost unjust, for Jesus to take compassion on me for being the only single person at a party. That he would meet me in the restroom after someone's backhanded comment has made me cry is absurd. Yet he introduces himself to the world with this miracle as someone very aware of the emotions associated with not meeting expectations, with being different, with wanting what other people have and not getting it. He knows exactly how it feels, and as shocking as it is, he cares. Jesus actually sees the mini trials you and I face. I hope you feel comforted by this.

But still, what if it never happens? It's comforting to hear that Jesus cares and knows and all that, but the question we're all really asking is, Will he provide? He can love me in the meantime, but is there an *end* to this phase? As Charlotte so perfectly put it in a scene from *Sex and the City*, "I have been dating since I was fifteen and I'm exhausted. Where is he?!" Can you and I be sure "the one" will actually appear someday?

After a particularly bad fight with Jake, I met my dad for dinner. In general I try to keep a strong face with my family, but on this night I just couldn't. I was in deep pain, terrified, and convinced that my whole life was going wrong. I didn't know how to express all of this, especially while choking on tears. So in what must have sounded like my voice at age six, I asked my dad, "Am I going to be okay?"

For the first time in my life I was past the point of knowing the answer. My ability to look down the road and believe everything would work out was gone. My dad paused, and I'm sure it broke his heart to say it, but he was honest with me: "Be okay? If you mean get married, I can't promise you that you will. I think it is likely that you will, but not for sure."

He was quiet as I tried very hard not to fall apart at the table. And then he said something I'll never forget: "But I know you will be okay, Cindy. Your life will be okay."

There are a lot of opinions on this subject, but after reflection, I have come to the same hard conclusion. I don't see how you and I can be absolutely sure that God will provide a spouse for every single person who wants one. God receives all kinds of prayers desperately requesting food, shelter, and healing. In his providence, he sometimes says no. As much as I would like to, I can't come up with a reason why a relationship request would be any different. God hears the prayers of his people but still allows hard times. Jesus even tells us to expect them.

So, what then? "What can we trust God for?" becomes the better question. Sadly, I believe church culture has promised lots of things God never promised. While these words of hope often come from a very loving place, they aren't always helpful in the long run.

Bad Promise Number 1

If you aren't called to the single life, you won't be single forever.

A myth pervading many Christian circles says that if you aren't *called* to the single life, then you won't be single forever. I wish (more than you know) I could say that you and I are going to get married because we want it, that "God wouldn't place the desire in our hearts if he wasn't going to fill it." But unfortunately, I've seen plenty of people end up in painful circumstances they weren't notified they were being called to.

We all have desires that go unmet. Nowhere in the Bible do I see a promise for getting everything we want in this life. How could this issue be any different? Can God individually make promises to people telling them they should trust him to provide something? Of course. (In fact, I'm kind of hoping

I get one of those.) But I don't think it's a blanket rule. I don't think one should expect it.

Bad Promise Number 2

In the meantime, God will be your perfect substitute.

Raise your hand if you've had someone tell you that you should focus on being the bride of Christ instead of worrying about finding a spouse. Keep that hand up if after expressing your desire for a spouse, you've been told that Jesus will meet your every need. These statements hold truth when used in the right context. Out of context, they don't line up with reality. For example, when we tell fatherless children that God wants to be their perfect and loving Father, we aren't saying that God is going to pick them up from practice or sit on their bed and talk them through a tough decision. When we tell an amputee that God will meet all their needs, we aren't saying he is necessarily going to choose to miraculously grow their leg back. We aren't saying a close relationship with God will feel and function as a missing parent or limb. What we are trying to say is that God wants to provide other greater needs.

In the same way, Jesus isn't going to be your husband. He isn't going to meet your real and normal needs (like provide a ride to the airport, be someone to have children with, or kill spiders for you) as a perfect (*perfect* meaning "exact") substitute. It doesn't work like that.

Promising what God hasn't exactly promised is harmful because it can make us mad at God for not coming through. When we expect him to show up in a way we shouldn't, it's easy to become angry or bitter with God or the church when it doesn't work out.

We grow frustrated with ourselves because we think (or are told) that we need to trust God more so that he'll come through for us. The logic goes something like, "*If* only I were closer to God and trusted him more, *then* I would experience the promise he made." Or in other words, "Great, now I'm single, God isn't who I thought he was, and oh, by the way, I'm not a good enough Christian either."

Bad Promise Number 3

God is keeping you single because he's working on your character. Translation: If you were a better person, you'd be married.

It's true that valuable spiritual growth and personal development can take place during singleness. You and I simply have fewer people depending on us, and this affords us certain opportunities we might not otherwise have. But to say that is *why* God is keeping you single is tricky. It *could* be. God can use whatever he wants to draw people to himself, but it would be a hard thing to prove as the ultimate reason.

No one is perfect. Every married person met their spouse without first learning certain lessons or growing in different ways. God is most likely hoping to grow them *in* marriage. There is no reason to believe he wouldn't want to do the same for us one day. And in this line of thinking, when would it end? Exactly what lesson do I need to learn before I can get married? Is it when I master patience? When I stop gossiping once and for all? How about when I've sold all of my personal items and rid myself of covetousness? Then will God bring me a husband?

This type of thinking is not only frustrating, but it incites guilt and motivates personal growth for the wrong reasons. It reads like God is playing some type of reward game with us, and that doesn't sound like him. He's our heavenly Father, who likes to give his children good and perfect gifts at just the right time. He gives out of who he is, not because of how well we perform.

A Better Train of Thought

In the end, wondering whether we will marry, whether we should marry, or how it will happen all end up being the wrong questions to start with. It isn't the best use of our time to try to figure it all out, as if there were some mystery to solve. God didn't create the earth as a setting for our romance stories. He didn't create you and me primarily to be someone's great love. As C. S. Lewis put it in *Mere Christianity*, "Being in love is a good thing, but it is not the best thing. There are many things below it, but there are also things above it. You cannot make it the basis of a whole life."

This might disappoint you (since it goes wildly against all the TV, movies, and novels we fill ourselves with), but I hope it frees you a little too. If our primary purpose were to be in a marital relationship, we'd all be failing at the moment. The truth that we weren't created first and foremost to be someone's wife or mother means we aren't missing the boat. It means there is nothing wrong with us.

What is God's purpose for us? God's priority seems to be

having a loving relationship with him and other people. You and I have the opportunity to be about so much more than our own lives. We get to partner in bringing peace, love, and hope to a world in need. We get to help right wrongs, heal hearts, and comfort the hurting. We get to know Jesus. That is God's priority for our lives. Single or married.

Being single is not who I am. Being single is just a context I am living in. Lately I've been thinking about what to do with my singleness as a commodity. How does God want me to use this phase of life? What about being single helps me live out his purpose for my life at this moment? The point of figuring out why I'm single changes from solving the why in order to meet someone, to solving the why so that my singleness can bless those around me.

I recently heard a sermon on giving that helped me put things in perspective. The text was Proverbs 3:9–10:

Honor the LORD with your wealth,
    with the firstfruits of all your crops;
then your barns will be filled to overflowing,
    and your vats will brim over with new wine.

—Proverbs 3:9–10

The goal is to honor the Lord with the firstfruits that come in during the first harvest. You give them before knowing whether more crops will come in, as opposed to comfortably after filling your plate. This demonstrates a heart of trust and an understanding that all things come from God. Firstfruits are the best fruits, not the moldy kind we don't really want anyway. This demonstrates that God holds the right priority in our lives.

When we give in this way, our barns and vats overflow. It's not a trick or an equation. It's not about giving a certain amount so that God will give us something back. Giving is a heart issue. With God, giving is always about generosity and a heart of trust.

Thinking of my singleness as something to be generous with has been extremely helpful for me. Living with a heart that is trusting God has given a purpose to my singleness. It's not about being good enough, joining ministries, or praying right so that God will bring me a husband. It's not about dating, trying eHarmony, or hitting the bar so that I take control. Losing weight, finding a hobby, or mastering the art of a first date isn't the be-all and end-all of existence. There are no hard and fast rules for what to do. *Whatever* I do in this phase, if done with a generous and trusting heart, I'll be doing the single thing right.

Thankfully, we don't need to beat ourselves up when we feel discontented either. We can be profoundly generous to someone else with our authenticity. God can use our frustrations and longings to speak to others. We can help those around us learn to live in the peace that comes from resting in God's promises to provide, even when we can't see the outcome.

Ultimately, we try to live generously so that a search for a husband doesn't become an idol. It is a lifelong battle to put God back in that number-one spot, to make our relationship with him our firstfruit. Everything around us sells the lie that our lives will be better if we find a man and that true happiness lies in that type of relationship. The best way I've found to avoid this trap is to consistently reorient the priorities of my heart. To regularly pray, "I'm sorry. I've done it again. I've made this romantic rat race my number-one priority. Forgive me. Help me to put you first. Help me to think about others more than myself." When I'm focused on being generous to others, I find I simply have less mental and emotional space for the other junk.

When my head hits the pillow at night, whether it's alone or with a husband, I want to have lived with a generous spirit. Out of this posture I will live out God's purpose for my life and for the world. I'm created to honor God by being generous with my life — my heart, my words, my time, my gifts, and my flaws. I believe this is my response, even if "it" never happens.

I wanted so desperately for my dad to say what I wanted to hear that night when I asked him if I was going to get married. In that broken state, I would've believed him had he said yes, the way little girls always believe their dads. But instead he gave me honesty. Which in the grand scheme of things, I appreciate. He gave me something far more helpful than a false hope; he gave me ownership of my own life and reminded me that he believed I could do something great with it, marital status aside.

Part of living generously involves being generous to yourself. I believe this means living your life to the fullest instead of wasting time while you look for a spouse. Single or married, we are the stewards of our own lives. Waiting for a partner isn't a good excuse for killing the time we've been given.

My friend Kelly is a constant reminder of this to me. She is not married and works as a doctor in Los Angeles. Kelly is beautiful, has a smile that lights up a room, and owns fabulous purses. What amazes me about Kelly is that she doesn't just have a career but goes to concerts, leads a small group, and rallies for Vegas when duty calls. She lives her life. She wants to be married but is going after her own dreams in the meantime.

Kelly doesn't let her relationship status have the final say on her happiness. When I asked her about her journey, she responded, "I will be sad if it doesn't happen to me. But again, I would be sad if I were caught up in the wrong relationship as well. So sadness is relative. I'm happy with where I am now, and it's hard to say whether a relationship will really make me happier."

This mentality is part of the generous single life. We are adults; we have no one to blame but ourselves if we look back on this time and find it void of adventure and fulfillment. Kelly is a happiness maker. She goes and finds it for herself.

If you want to go back to school, I say do it. You aren't too old. If you want to be a painter, writer, or singer, work on your craft. If you want to travel in a foreign country, save for a ticket. It is your life. The best part of being single is just that—it is your life. You can do what you want without having to consider a spouse's plans and needs. Don't pass up the very best part of this whole deal simply because you wish you were married. Make sure you experience the good side.

I'm hoping the bad news that I don't believe everyone will for sure get married is softened by the good news that there is more to life than meeting someone, registering at Macy's, and posting homemade organic recipes on Instagram all day. Even if this particular desire goes unmet, there are plenty of other exciting things in life to experience.

As often as girlfriends and I talk about relationships, what continues to amaze me is that I wouldn't trade my years of singleness for anything in the world. I really wouldn't. If I could somehow go back in time, I still wouldn't have married in college, at twenty-five, or even at twenty-seven, because it would mean some of my best memories wouldn't have happened. I grew close friendships with my younger brothers, Mark and Matt, during my twenties. Mark and I lived for a summer in Costa Rica when I was twenty-six, and I was able to be at all of Matt's high school and college cross-country meets, dances, and graduations in part because I'm single. I ran a marathon that my dad, older brother, Tim, and sister-in-law Jenni helped train me for. I spent time hanging out with my mom and learned about cooking and hosting. I wouldn't want to have missed this time and wouldn't trade it for any man on the planet.

I've shared my single life with incredible friends. I've had the opportunity to take inner-city kids to see snow for the first time, cheer them through a ropes course at summer camp, and watch their faces as they realized God sees them and loves them. I've traveled through Latin America and Europe and written the book you're holding. I don't regret my adventures in dating, and I don't want to be married to any of my exes. I've become confident, independent, and beautiful in these last ten years, and I think the next ten will be all the better for it.

But ...

It would be really nice to have someone take care of me once in a while. Taking out the trash, calling the plumber, and bugging my dad to help me move out of my apartment every six months get old—for both of us. While I won't tell you that getting close to Jesus is the same as finding a husband, I will tell you he has a plan in place for this stuff too. It involves being a part of his family.

There is a group of people who usually hang out at church, and they are meant to be the hands and feet of Jesus. You and I need them. When I needed a place to grab dinner before a meeting, when my car battery died at work, and when it was time to look for a new job, these people showed up. My church has encouraged and affirmed me on a regular basis. They provide a place for me to be deeply known and loved many times over. And in the end, isn't this what we are looking for?

Whether we are married or single, we all want the same things. And it can be very painful to go without. At the time of the fall, in the middle of the punishment given to Eve, right after the pain of childbirth in Genesis 3, there is this fascinating line in verse 16: "'Your desire will be for your husband.'" When I came across it in college, a lightbulb went off in my head. *Oh my gosh! It's a freaking punishment!* This crazy feeling, this chasing after love, this sting of rejection—it's a punishment. And it feels like a punishment.

Just like God never promised that pushing a baby out would feel easy, he's not going to make the unmet desires of our hearts feel easy all the time either. Regardless of our relationship status, you and I are plagued with a desire for man in some form. Be it attention from strangers, the affection of a neglectful husband, or the adoration of an absent father, we want their love. And it's not going away. (Is that not the crappiest news ever? Sorry. At least it means you're not crazy.

That's something, right?) I believe one day God will wipe away every tear and our hearts will be fully mended. But we carry some form of this curse till then. We will always feel our needs go unmet in some fashion. We might as well be honest about it.

If we continue to seek Jesus, even with a disappointed and confused heart, our lives will be okay. If we keep going after the things we were wired and created to do, we will be okay. God never promised it would be easy. Maybe this is where the idea of becoming the bride of Christ actually makes sense—it's a for-better-and-for-worse relationship. You and I have to come to a place where we decide we will stick with him even when we are afraid we will never get the things we want—not pretend we don't have wants, but not become consumed by them either. We daily give them over to him and listen for what to do next.

What Are We Afraid Of?

When I was young and had nightmares, my mom and dad would come to my room and have me repeat the verse "perfect love casts out fear." I would repeat this until I fell asleep. For years, I would doze off saying, "Perfect love casts out fear; perfect love casts out fear; perfect love casts out fear."

The emotion I meet in my single friends more than any other is fear. When I'm having a bad day, fear is what is written on my heart. When I dread the future, fear is behind it. We are afraid marriage is never going to happen. We are afraid we are going to have to stay in this place of singleness for a long time. We are afraid we have somehow missed the plan God had for us. We are afraid everyone else is moving on and we are stuck, standing still. We are afraid it is our fault, that there is something wrong with us. We are afraid it is God's fault; he could change it if he wanted to, but he doesn't. We are afraid no one will ever love us and choose us. We are afraid there is no one left for us to love and to choose.

And our worst fear may come true. This is why we need perfect love. Love is what we are searching for in a spouse — to be loved and to have someone to love. We know in our heads that no man will fulfill every need, read our minds, and never let us down. Whether we're married or not, only Jesus can get inside our hearts and cast a light where it feels dark. Only his love is perfect. Only perfect love casts out fear. There is so much of Jesus to know, and at the end of the day, he's the only way out of the fear.

If you are like me, you probably swing from hopeful to hopeless, joyful to sad, grateful to bitter, lonely to full. This phase of life is inconsistent. There are extreme highs and extreme lows. So many things are outside of our control. Our timetables and goals have proved too hard to achieve. This is why sticking with Jesus is a good idea. Not because he is the same as a husband or boyfriend, not because religion solves your problems, not because your parents told you so. It's because he is faithful. He doesn't leave; he doesn't ignore; he doesn't reject. He doesn't change his mind or lack the ability to commit. It's quite the opposite. He stays; he listens; he chooses us and will never go back on his commitments. He offers us a future that begins right now.

We are all waiting on something, even when we try not to. We are waiting to meet the one, waiting to feel like we can start a life with someone, waiting to be loved and celebrated. Thank God a future with him starts today. He has a life planned for you right now, just as you are. He's not trying to rush you. He doesn't think you are behind.

When Jesus turned the water into wine, he revealed something about himself. By taking water used for ceremonial cleaning and turning it into the best wine, he illustrated that the old system of religion wasn't enough. Only a life with him could make a person brand new. Only his way of life would be truly fulfilling. For us, that relationship, that married life everyone else has, won't ultimately make us happy.

If you came to this book looking for answers, Jesus really is the only one I can offer. And honestly, it kind of bugs me to admit it. I wish I could come up with something brilliant and more tangible—some secret, fail-proof road map for surviving this time in our lives. I wish I had excellent tips for getting over a broken heart or where to meet men who are worth finding. But deep down, I believe you are too smart to buy any of that crap anyway. You know all advice falls short at some point.

You understand that part of the beauty of life is that everyone's story is a little different, and only someone as complicated, miraculous, and winsome as Jesus can give true life. It's not the same life, exactly, as the one we may want right now, but it can be exciting and fulfilling. And no matter what, you and I will be okay.

Notes

1. United States Census Bureau, "Figure 1. Median Age at First Marriage by Sex: 1890 to 2010," *https://www.census.gov/hhes/socdemo/marriage/data/acs/ElliottetalPAA2012figs.pdf.*

2. Lecture by Dr. David Spiegel, director of the Center on Stress and Health, professor in the School of Medicine, associate chair of Stanford University School of Medicine — Psychiatry and Behavioral Sciences.

3. David Kinnaman, with Aly Hawkins, *You Lost Me: Why Young Christians Are Leaving Church … and Rethinking Faith* (Grand Rapids, Mich.: Baker, 2011), 150.

4. ChristianMingle.com and JDate.com, "2014 State of Dating in America," *http://www.stateofdatingreport.com/findings.htm.*

5. National Campaign to Prevent Teen and Unplanned Pregnancy, 2009, *http://thenationalcampaign.org/.*